The flames were growing stronger and spreading swiftly toward the front of the house. Michelle raced back to the porch. The door was open a crack now and she could see Dana's hand.

"Can you open the door any wider?" Michelle asked her.

"The bookcase fell against it. I can't get out!"

"Barney, come help me!"

When he didn't answer, Michelle put her back against the door and pushed as hard as she could. It moved only an inch or two. "Can you open the window bars from the inside?"

"I can't get up. I've hurt my foot. Michelle!" she shrieked. "Flames! I'm going to burn!"

by Alida E. Young

Willowisp
Press®

*This book is dedicated to my family,
who always gives me encouragement and support.*

*Special thanks to my son Ben, who helps critique
my stories. Many thanks for their invaluable help
to Anita Arrington, R.N. B.S.N. at Hi-Desert
Medical Center; Joyce A. Babyak, director of
Volunteer Services at Eisenhower Medical Center;
Reanna Howell at Eisenhower; Amy, Beverly, and
Dan Schick; and Dr. Klonda Bell. And to Laura
Belgrave, my editor, who two days before the huge
earthquake hit near my town said, "Why don't you
start the story with a quake!"*

Cover design by Michael Petty

Published by Willowisp Press
801 94th Avenue North, St. Petersburg, Florida 33702

Copyright © 1993 by Willowisp Press,
a division of PAGES, Inc.

Printed in the United States of America

2 4 6 8 10 9 7 5 3 1

ISBN 0-87406-660-3

One

MICHELLE De Berg pushed open the carved wooden door of her father's Spanish-style office and stepped inside the air-conditioned room.

His nurse-receptionist, Edith, looked up. "Hello, love. Your dad's with a patient. He's—"

She stopped as the floor began to vibrate. "Uh-oh, here it comes!"

Michelle dropped her tennis racket and grabbed the sides of the doorway to brace herself.

"How'd you like that one?" Edith asked when the rumbling stopped.

"I hardly notice these little earthquakes." Michelle grinned. "The washing machine shakes our house worse than that."

"Well I, for one, don't like them."

Michelle chuckled. "My friend Dana hasn't

lived in southern California very long, and she goes ape whenever we have a little quake. I think she believes all that crazy talk about California breaking off and falling into the ocean. Well, I'd rather be in an earthquake than a tornado or a hurricane."

"I'll pass on all of them, thank you very much," Edith said.

Michelle picked up her racket. "How long will Dad be? We have the court reserved for 5:30."

"He's running late," said Edith. "He was called to an emergency at the hospital, so his office appointments got backed up."

Dr. Michael De Berg had been running late since he was named chief of staff at Palm Grove hospital. He only kept the Santa Reyes office open two days a week, and on those days his patient schedule was heavy.

"So, how's it feel to be out of school?" Edith asked.

"Great. The last few weeks were murder, though. Most days the temperature was around 110, and can you believe our gym teacher made us run a mile in that heat?"

"Life's rough." Edith smiled sympathetically. "What are your plans for the rest of the summer? Your dad said you might join the junior volunteer program at the hospital."

The hospital. Michelle hated it. Her stomach knotted the way it did whenever she remembered watching her mother die of cancer. Turning quickly away, she closed her eyes. She dug her fingers into her palm, trying to block the painful memories. It didn't help. Nothing ever helped. Nothing ever stopped the nightmares.

Mama, why did you have to leave me?

Every day for weeks she had gone to her mother's hospital room. Her beautiful mother, so thin and frail. The smell of sickness in the room. Medicines. Tubes in her nose and her arms.

Michelle shuddered. How could she tell her father that just the thought of the hospital brought the pain back?

"Honey, are you all right?" Edith asked.

"Sure." Michelle turned around and forced a smile. "I think I'll be doing something else this summer. Dana and I are trying to save enough money to go to Hawaii while Dad's at his medical convention."

As Michelle picked up a magazine from a wrought iron table, her father emerged with a patient, a young woman in tears. "But Doctor De, I can't pay—"

7

"Now, don't you worry, Mrs. Johnson," he said, cutting her off. "We'll figure out something." As he led the woman to the door, he focused his entire attention on her.

Michelle shook her head. Her dad was something else. If somebody needed help, even a stranger, he'd come to the rescue. She wished he were there for her just as readily.

When he finally turned around and saw Michelle, he smiled broadly. Michelle couldn't help but smile back. It struck her that he was not only the most caring doctor in town, he was also the best-looking. With his curly brown hair and electric blue eyes, he looked more like a movie star than a doctor.

"Hi, honey, what's up?" he asked.

Michelle groaned. "You've forgotten, haven't you?"

Dr. De Berg glanced at the tennis racket and grimaced. "Honey, I'm sorry. Dr. Fisher asked me to fill in for him at the clinic tonight. I'll be late."

"Why can't someone else do that? Why does it always have to be you?" Michelle fingered the sign-in clipboard. "Maybe if I made an appointment, I'd get to see more of you." She said it jokingly, trying not to let her hurt show.

"Sweetheart, we'll do something this weekend. I prom—"

"You've promised that every weekend for a month," she said, fighting tears.

As she hurried out the door, she heard him say, "Edith, do all fourteen-year-olds act like this?"

*   *   *   *   *

Michelle hated the thought of going home to an empty house. Mrs. Peterson, the housekeeper, would have left for the day. Even her Siamese cat Mookie would probably be asleep. Still hurt, she walked the few blocks to the mall and called Dana. It took a little coaxing, but Dana agreed to meet Michelle at The Pig Out, their favorite gourmet dessert shop. They could go over their Hawaii plans.

At The Pig Out, Michelle took a booth and ordered their usual: cheesecake with chocolate chips and macadamia nuts. She knew she should save her money for the trip, but she figured she deserved something special today.

She was daydreaming of white sands and coral reefs when Dana Chang arrived.

"I ordered for both of us," Michelle said as Dana slid into the booth.

"What's the occasion? I thought you were playing ten—"

"I don't want to talk about it."

"Uh-oh," Dana said softly. "Your dad stood you up again, huh?"

"Oh, he couldn't help it." Michelle avoided her friend's eyes. "He had to fill in at the clinic." She added wistfully, "It's just not fair." She crumbled a paper napkin and sighed. "I know I shouldn't gripe, but I'd just like to see him once in a while—you know?"

Dana nodded. "Well, maybe he won't be so busy at the hospital this summer."

That was true, Michelle thought, feeling a little better. Many of her father's patients were retirees who abandoned the desert the minute it got hot.

When the waitress brought the cheese-cakes, Dana took the first bite and gave a little moan of delight. "They should call this Velvet Heaven."

"Speaking of heaven," said Michelle, "did you bring the travel stuff about Hawaii?"

Dana's great-uncle had invited them to spend two weeks at his condo in Lahaina, Maui. All Michelle needed was airfare.

"Uncle Yee sent some brochures," Dana said, spreading them out on the table. But her voice lacked enthusiasm.

"It's going to be great, Dana," said Michelle. "We can meet guys, snorkel, meet guys, explore caves, meet guys, and stay in the ocean until we turn into prunes." She grinned playfully. "Oh, yes, and meet incredibly gorgeous guys."

Dana said nothing.

"I can't wait to get out of Santa Reyes," Michelle said. "It's not quite July and it's supposed to get to 117 tomorrow."

Dana reached back and twisted her long hair into a silky knot. "I think I'll cut my hair. It would be so much cooler."

Michelle knew it was an idle threat. For both of them, their hair was their best feature.

"I guess you know it'll be hot in Hawaii, too," Dana said.

Dana had moved from Canada a few years before and still wasn't used to the dry desert heat. The two had become best friends almost immediately, maybe because they were such opposites. Dana was tiny, amber-skinned, and fragile-looking; Michelle was tall and fair. Dana disliked sports; Michelle was athletic. Dana was neat and methodical, and worried about nearly everything; Michelle never planned ahead, and took things as they came. Both Mrs. Peterson and her dad considered her downright irresponsible. To prove otherwise, Michelle was doing her best to earn her own money for the trip.

"At least you don't have to worry about sunburn," Michelle said. She had the translucent skin that usually went with red-gold hair. Her mother, whose coloring had been the same, used to say she could get a sunburn from a night-light.

"Mom says you can burn twice as easily in the tropics," Dana said.

"Well, I'm not going to worry about it. Are your parents going to pay for you to go?" Michelle asked, leafing through the pictures of the islands.

"Yes. How much have you saved?"

"About sixty bucks. I got twenty-five for the last babysitting job. But all my regulars are leaving for the summer. I hope I can save enough by August."

"Maybe we should just wait until next year," Dana said. "We'll have more time to plan."

"Plan? I'm ready to leave tomorrow," said Michelle. Then a thought struck her. "Are you trying to back out?"

"Nooo . . . I just wish there was another way to get to Hawaii besides on a plane. I hate flying."

Michelle muttered, "If we don't go to Hawaii, this will be the most boring summer in history."

"We could volunteer at the hospital," Dana said hesitantly.

"Are you on that thing again?" Michelle couldn't tell her friend the real reason she didn't want to be a volunteer. "Only nerds volunteer." She eyed Dana suspiciously. "Has my dad been after you?"

"No. And you're wrong about junior volunteers being nerds. Travis Knight is a volunteer, and he's the most popular guy in town. And what about Amber Berenson? She's certainly no nerd."

"I think you just want an excuse to be around Travis. But I've told you a million times I don't want to have anything to do with the hospital. Anyway, I'd never be any good in an emergency."

"Who says? We could just try it. Maybe you could see more of your dad if you're both working at the hospital."

Michelle had to admit that would certainly be true. But she didn't want to give up on Hawaii, and without Dana she'd never get there. Her dad would never let her go alone, and certainly not without someplace to stay. No, she had to convince Dana to go.

While they ate, Michelle continued to bombard her friend with the wonders of the islands.

Finally, Dana said, "Okay, okay. You win. I'll go." She picked at the cheesecake with her fork.

"You won't be sorry," Michelle said quickly. "It'll be the best vacation we—"

A sudden jolt shook the booth. Glasses rattled. The floor shuddered.

Dana screamed, "Earthquake!"

Two

DANA dove under the booth. Michelle gripped the edge of the table. Her glass of water had tipped over, scattering pieces of ice. Behind the counter, dishes shattered. Outside in the mall, the water in the fountain sloshed from side to side. People ran from windows and the concrete overhangs.

Then, as suddenly as it had begun, the shaking stopped.

The waitress asked if everyone was all right. She appeared almost undisturbed. This was just another California shaker.

Slowly, an ashen-faced Dana emerged from beneath the table and slumped into her seat. Her voice trembled as she whispered, "Is it over?"

"Hey, it's okay." Michelle mopped up water with napkins. She smiled reassuringly. "That was nothing."

"I don't know how you can be so calm."

"If you live in southern California, you have to expect a few quakes. You'll get used to them."

"Ha! Francine is even more scared than I am and she's lived here for years."

"Your grandmother would be afraid of Bambi."

Everybody called Dana's grandmother Francine. Michelle thought it was weird, but that was the way she wanted it.

"Francine thinks the 'Big One' will hit us hard. This one was bad enough to suit me."

Michelle had to admit the quake was stronger than any they had experienced for a while. She didn't want to upset Dana, but depending on where the epicenter was, there could be some damage.

The waitress tuned the radio to the station in the larger town of Palm Grove. A reporter broke into the music. "Southern California just experienced a moderate earthquake. We're trying to reach Cal Tech for more information."

Dana pushed aside the rest of her cheesecake. "Let's get out of here."

Michelle stuffed down another bite, then quickly dug in her pocket for her share of the bill. "Hey, I'm sorry, Dana.

I forgot my money."

"You can pay me back, but I wish you'd remember for a change."

Michelle ignored the remark. Dana was just upset.

Once outside the mall, Dana said, "How about sleeping over tonight?" She still sounded a bit shaken.

"I really ought to go home and check on Mookie. She's probably hiding. The last time we had a quake, that crazy cat shot across the room like a bullet and hit me in the chest. Nearly knocked me over."

"Okay, but will you walk home with me?"

"There's no reason to be scared, Dana. Your apartment is new. They're all required to be built to earthquake codes. It would take a lot more than that little shake to knock it down."

"So you're saying that it's strong enough to stand up against the 'Big One' everybody talks about? You know, the one that's supposed to happen on the San Andreas Fault?"

All her life, Michelle had heard about the notorious San Andreas Fault, the eight-hundred-mile rupture in the earth's crust from northern California to the Salton Sea in the south end of the state. She wasn't at all certain that *any* building could

17

withstand the huge quake seismologists predicted would happen in the next thirty years.

But thirty years was a lifetime away. Why panic now?

"You're such a worrywart, Dana," Michelle said. "Come on, I'll walk you home."

On the way, Michelle changed the subject back to Hawaii. "I hope we can ride in an outrigger canoe and go to a luau. I want to learn to dance the hula."

Dana offered a few other ideas in return. She seemed more enthusiastic than before. *Maybe*, Michelle thought, *Dana feared earthquakes more than airplanes*.

At the Royal Dunes apartments, Dana again asked her to sleep over.

"Your mom and dad will be home, won't they?" Michelle asked.

"Yes, but they'll probably work late at the paper on account of the earthquake."

Mr. Chang was editor of the *Santa Reyes Review*, a local newspaper that came out three times a week. Mrs. Chang worked in the paper's business office.

"Look, let me check on Mookie. If she's okay, I'll leave a note for Dad and ride back here on my bike."

"You promise? I know you. You'll get to

hunting for Mookie or listening to music and forget all about coming back."

"I won't forget. I promise."

On the way home to get her bike, Michelle took a shortcut. It would be dark soon, and she didn't want to ride along stretches of unlighted road.

The shortcut took her through an old neighborhood of crumbling stucco houses, boarded-up buildings, and a few businesses, most of which were closed for the day. The quake had obviously been stronger here. People were sweeping up broken glass or boarding up storefront windows or standing around in little groups, listening to radios.

On the outskirts of the neighborhood the sidewalk abruptly ended, and Michelle had to make her way along a sandy path. In this area of town, there were no palm trees or watered lawns and gardens. The desert had returned, staking its claim with creosote bushes and tumbleweed.

Michelle began to walk faster. Santa Reyes had little crime, but her dad would pitch a fit if he knew she was alone here. She felt uneasy. Maybe Dana's fears had rubbed off on her.

Cut it out, she told herself sternly. *After all, you took a karate class.* But she couldn't

19

block the rest of the thought: *You also quit after the first week.*

A strange noise intruded on her thoughts. Michelle stopped and looked around. A hurt animal? Maybe a cat? She heard it again. The sound seemed to come from a square cement-block building that looked like a deserted repair shop. Rusty broken cars sat in the yard.

Slowly, Michelle walked toward the building. The sound was louder now. Something was definitely in trouble. As she got closer, the cry seemed more human than animal, and she ran across the sand, almost stumbling over an old metal car bumper.

One of the two garage doors was open. Michelle peered inside the dark building. It smelled of must and oil and smoke.

"Is anyone in here?"

A groan came from the back.

Guided by faint light coming from the rear of the building, Michelle stepped inside. As she walked toward the back she realized the building wasn't deserted after all. The light revealed a cot, a table made from a crate, an overturned car seat, and a small charcoal barbecue. Then she saw that the light was coming from a break in the masonry wall and part of the roof.

"Help us," a weak voice gasped.

Michelle quickened her steps, stumbling over chunks of concrete. An old man lay crumpled on the floor behind the car seat. His face looked gray, and he was gripping his chest.

Panicked, Michelle looked around, wondering what she should do. She knelt beside the man. His breathing sounded shallow and strained. "Don't worry," she said in a shaky voice. "I'll get help." She stood and turned to leave.

The old man shook his head. "No, no! Emilio!" he gasped. "Help . . . my boy."

At first Michelle didn't see the child. He lay almost completely covered by rubble. But a new moan drew her eyes to him. She caught her breath. Blood seeped from his forehead and his arm. His eyes were closed, but he was moaning softly. He was alive.

Frantically, Michelle began to pull off chunks of concrete. As she uncovered his legs, the sight made her sick and she gagged. One leg was at an odd angle, and a broken bone poked through the skin.

The boy opened his eyes, looked up at her for a second, then whispered something that sounded like "on-hell" or "ong-hell."

Michelle shook her head, not understanding. "I'm sorry. I—"

"On-hell, On-hell!" he cried, grasping her arm.

Knowing she had to get help, Michelle tried to pull away, but the boy hung on. His dark eyes stared into hers. "On-hell," he said again, his voice almost reverent.

He must be almost out of his mind with pain, she thought. Gently, she pulled away. "I'll be right back," she said. "I promise."

"He's hurt bad," she told the old man. "I have to get help."

She raced toward the neighborhood stores and stopped a woman on the street. "Phone? Where's the nearest phone?"

The woman shook her head as if she didn't understand English. Frustrated, Michelle raced on. She found a small grocery store at the end of the block. The storekeeper was picking up broken glass and cans that had fallen from the shelves.

"I need a phone!" she said breathlessly.

The storekeeper's eyes shot up.

"A little boy is crushed under some concrete," Michelle continued. "An old man is hurt too! They're in a deserted building that looks like an auto shop of some kind. Part of the wall and roof fell in."

The storekeeper quickly pointed to a

phone at the end of the counter.

As Michelle dialed 911, people from the neighborhood gathered around her. "We need an ambulance!" she said into the phone. She quickly described the conditions of the old man and the boy. "Please hurry!"

The storekeeper took the phone and gave directions. He hung up and turned to Michelle. "The old man and the boy must be Ruben Garcia and his grandson Emilio. They've been living in that condemned building."

"We'd better get them out of there," another man said. "Joe? Bill? Let's go."

"I'll show you where," Michelle said. On the way, she asked, "Why were those two living in that place?"

"I'm not sure, but from what I understand, they used to live in Los Angeles," one of the men said.

When they reached the building, they found that the old man had lapsed into unconsciousness. The boy, who appeared to be six or seven, was quiet now. Almost afraid to go near him, Michelle held back while one of the men knelt down beside him.

"I don't think we'd better move the kid," the man said. "Somebody find a blanket."

A woman who had accompanied the group was tending to the old man. "He's probably had a heart attack or a stroke. He seems to be breathing okay."

The boy began to moan and writhe, his face twisting with pain. "On-hell? On-hell?" he cried.

Michelle moved slowly toward him. When he saw her, his facial muscles relaxed. "On-hell." With great effort he held out his hand.

"What's he saying?" she asked the man. "He must think I'm his mother or something."

"Not his mother. With that reddish-gold hair of yours, he thinks you're an angel."

"You're kid—" She saw by his face that he was serious.

"Go on," the man said. "Take his hand while we wait for the ambulance. You seem to calm him down."

Michelle sat on the hard concrete floor, holding the boy's cold hand. Even though she didn't know him, she felt as if there were a bond between them.

She hadn't prayed since her mother died. It hadn't done any good then, but maybe she hadn't prayed hard enough. Her lips moved silently: *Please don't let this little boy die.*

Three

THE siren grew closer and stopped outside. Paramedics hurried in. They quickly checked the boy for bleeding, then immediately started tending the old man. As soon as they had the man stabilized, they returned to the boy.

When Michelle tried to pull her hand free so she'd be out of the way, the boy began to cry and thrash about.

"You'd better stay where you are, Miss," one of the paramedics said. "At least until we get his leg taken care of."

Michelle remained, but she had to look away.

The little boy cried out and gripped her hand tightly. She found herself murmuring, "Shh, shh . . . don't cry, Emilio. You're going to be all right."

She felt his hand relax a little. She wasn't

sure if her words had helped or not. Maybe it was something the paramedics had given him for pain. But when the paramedics tried to put him onto a gurney, the boy still refused to let go of her.

One of the neighborhood men said, "Why don't you let the girl go to the hospital with him?"

Michelle felt panic set in. The hospital was the last place in the world she wanted to be. Only when one of the paramedics explained that it would be against policy for her to ride along did she begin to relax—but only for a moment. The boy, despite his groggy condition, was watching her with his great dark eyes. She couldn't look away.

Maybe, Michelle thought, *it wouldn't really hurt to ride along to the hospital.* By the time they arrived, Emilio would probably be asleep and unaware if she was there or not.

"My dad's Dr. De Berg, chief of staff," she blurted. "I'm sure he'll see that you don't get into any trouble."

Reluctantly, the paramedics agreed to let her go along.

The nine-mile ride to Palm Grove seemed to take forever. Finally, they pulled into the emergency entrance. The boy was moaning softly, his eyes closed.

"You'll have to stay in the waiting room," a paramedic told her.

"But I'm not a relative or anything," Michelle protested. "I've never even seen them before."

Emilio still kept a firm grip on Michelle's hand. As before, when she tried to draw away, he began to cry and tried to raise himself up.

"I'm sorry, but I can't go in with you," she told him.

"Please, will you wait?" Mr. Garcia said to her, getting more agitated himself. "I wish to thank you properly."

Michelle looked at the hospital—the same hospital where her mother had died. She took a deep, quivering breath. "All right. I'll hang around for a while."

"Bless you," the old man whispered.

She watched the paramedics roll the gurneys into the emergency room. "I hope they'll both be okay," she said half-aloud.

In the waiting room, she called the clinic where her father had said he would be filling in. A recorded voice said it was closed.

Next, she tried the house. Her father answered with a brusque "De Berg residence."

"Dad, it's me."

"Michelle! Are you all right?"

"I'm fine. I'm—"

"Where in blazes are you? After the quake, I tried to find you. I was just getting ready to call the police."

"I'm at the hospital." She explained about finding Mr. Garcia and Emilio. "The darned kid wouldn't let me go," she said, half-proud, half-resentful of having to be in this place she hated.

"What were you doing in that part of town?" he exploded. "I've told you a million—" He took a deep breath. "I'm sorry, honey. I was just so worried about you. When Dana said you'd promised to—"

"Dana! I forgot all about her. I'd better call her too."

"All right. I'll let you go. But I'll be there in a few minutes," he said.

Dana answered on the first ring. "Where are you? Your dad's been wild."

"I'm fine. He's picking me up here in Palm Grove—at the hospital."

"The hospital? Are you okay? Was there an accident? What—"

"No, nothing like that." Michelle didn't want to go through the story again. "It's a long story. I'll tell you all about it tomorrow."

"Tomorrow! You said you were coming here tonight. You promised."

"I know I did, but—" Michelle glanced at the clock on the wall. "It's after eight-thirty now. I don't know how soon we'll get back to Santa Reyes. You're okay, aren't you?"

"I am now," Dana said sullenly. "Can't you tell me what's going on?"

"I've got to get off the phone. I'll come over first thing in the morning."

"Okay, but sometimes you drive me nuts, Michelle. I hate to think what kind of mess you're in now."

For the first time since she'd found the Garcias, Michelle laughed. "I'm not in a mess. Actually, I played the Good Samaritan this evening." With that little teaser, she said goodbye and hung up.

A senior volunteer at the desk smiled at her. Michelle could understand why older people volunteered; they probably needed things to keep them busy. But why anyone wanted to be a junior volunteer was beyond her.

It seemed like forever before she saw her father stride through the doors. He hurried over and gave her a bear hug. "I swear, you're going to give me gray hair."

"I'm sorry, but this time it's not my fault."

Before he could start to lecture her again, she said, "Dad, can you find out how the Garcias are doing? I promised I'd wait to talk to the grandfather."

"I'm going to look in on a couple of my patients and see if the earthquake upset them. After that I'll check on the Garcias."

He gave her another hug. "Honey, I'm really proud of you. Not everybody acts well under pressure, but you did. You may very well have saved their lives. I told you you'd make a good volunteer." Then he added, "But I still don't want you wandering around alone in that part of town."

"Dad, you should have seen the place they were living. It was a condemned building. No water. No toilet. Nothing. I didn't know people had to live like that. Not in Santa Reyes, anyhow. Can you do anything to help them?"

"We'll see. A lot of homeless people are moving out of the city. I'm glad you're developing a social conscience." With a wave, her father headed for the elevator.

The minutes dragged as she waited for him to return. When he was working, he lost all sense of time. It was after ten o'clock when he returned. Michelle didn't like the somber expression on his face.

"What's happened? Are Mr. Garcia and Emilio okay?"

"The boy came through the surgery all right, but Garcia had another mild heart attack. They're both in the critical care unit."

"There's more, isn't there?" she asked softly.

He nodded. "I'm sorry, honey. The boy has compound fractures of the lower leg, but even worse, the arteries were crushed. I'm afraid there's a chance that Emilio may lose a leg."

Michelle's eyes stung with tears. She kept shaking her head. "But he's just a little boy," she whispered.

"Come on, honey, we'd better get home."

"I promised I'd wait." She sighed. "Mr. Garcia wants to talk to me."

"Not tonight. He isn't able to talk to anyone."

Secretly, Michelle felt relief wash over her. She should never have said she'd stay.

But as she and her father were driving home, she couldn't quite shake the image of the little boy's hand tugging hers, and the way he thought she was an angel. Crazy kid . . .

Four

"ANYTHING on the radio about the earthquake?" Michelle asked her father the next morning.

Mrs. Peterson had called to say she didn't feel well, so Michelle was fixing strawberries and muffins for breakfast.

"Not much," her father replied. He took a sip of coffee and made a face.

Michelle hadn't bothered to read the instruction book for the coffeemaker. She had guessed how much coffee to use. Obviously, she had guessed wrong.

"Two houses were destroyed in Palm Grove," he went on. "There was some minor damage in the old part of Santa Reyes."

How could you call it "minor damage" when a little boy might lose a leg? Michelle thought to herself. "When you make your rounds this morning, would you check on the Garcias for me?" she asked.

"If they're doing better, maybe I can arrange for you to see them for a few minutes this afternoon."

It was one thing to sit in the emergency waiting room. But the thought of going into the critical care unit made Michelle feel queasy. "No, that's okay," she said quickly. "I have a lot of things to do and—"

The phone cut her off. "I'll get it," she said, jumping up, glad for any excuse to change the subject. She was even more glad to hear Dana's voice.

"Hi, Dana, what's up?"

"Did you take the brochures on Hawaii with you yesterday?" Dana asked.

"No. I thought you took them. They're probably still at The Pig Out."

"I called last evening. They haven't seen them. Are you *sure* you didn't take them?" Dana asked. "Are you trying to use reverse psychology on me to get me to Hawaii?"

"Of course not," Michelle said irritably. "You already said you'd go. Anyway, what's the big deal? Can't your uncle just send more?"

"I guess," Dana said, sighing. A long pause followed. "You *are* coming over, aren't you? I'm dying to know what

33

happened last night."

"I'll be there in a little while."

"Well, don't be too long," Dana said crossly. "It seems like I'm always waiting around for you."

Michelle rolled her eyes. What was Dana's problem, anyhow? "I'll get there as soon as I can," she said.

When she returned to the table, her father studied her carefully. "What was all that about Dana's uncle? You're not still talking about Hawaii, are you?"

"You said I could go if I proved I'm responsible," said Michelle. "Well, I'm doing that. I'm earning the money myself. I'm going to keep my room clean from now on and—"

"After that stunt you pulled last night, I think you have more to prove to me than that," said her father. He put down his coffee cup and frowned. "You've been told to stay out of that part of town. You went into a condemned building. If there had been an aftershock, you could have been killed."

"Last night you said you were proud of me."

"Well, I still am, but I couldn't sleep last night, thinking about what could have happened."

"You'd have done the same thing," Michelle said, a little belligerently.

"Of course I would. I'm a doctor, and—" Her father stopped and cleared his throat, as if suddenly aware of how feeble his argument must sound. "Anyway, you talk big about responsibility. You told me you felt responsible for the Garcias, but you don't even want to see for yourself how they're doing."

"And they say mothers know how to make kids feel guilty," Michelle mumbled.

"I'm sorry, honey. That wasn't fair." Her father sighed. "About Hawaii. I just wish I knew what your mother would say about letting you go three thousand miles away."

"She'd say, 'It will be a wonderful learning experience for you, Michelle. Have a great time, dear, and bring me back an orchid lei. But wear a sun hat and sunscreen and watch out for sharks!'"

Her father laughed—the first joyous sound Michelle had heard him make in connection with her mother's memory. He got up, came around the table, and gave Michelle a hug.

"If I seem hard on you sometimes, it's only because I love you." He glanced at his watch. "I've got to go. Tonight we'll go out for pizza. No, wait. I can't. I have a meeting at the hospital." He dug a bill out of his wallet and tossed it on the table. "I'm sorry, honey, but you'll have to order out."

Michelle watched her father leave. *He says he loves me, so how come he never has any time for me?*

As she started to clear the table, the cat rubbed up against her leg. "Mookie, you must be starved. Last night was so weird, I forgot all about feeding you."

Suddenly, the cat seemed to freeze in place. She stared straight ahead, her hair on end.

"What's wro—" And then Michelle felt it. The floor trembled. The warm coffee in the cup splashed on her hand. The dishes in the cupboards rattled.

Michelle let her breath out slowly. "Don't worry, Mookie, that was just a little bitty aftershock. Nothing to worry about."

* * * * *

Michelle pushed the elevator button for the fifth floor. She was tempted to take the stairs to the Changs' apartment. After all, an elevator was the last place she wanted to be in an earthquake. But as she'd told

Dana, the building was built to strict earthquake codes. She pushed from her mind Dana's question: "But what about the 'Big One'?"

The Changs were just finishing lunch. Michelle liked Dana's parents because they always seemed interested in what she had to say. Maybe that came from being newspaper people.

"I thought you were coming over this morning," Dana said, sounding cross. "Did you forget—again?"

"No, but I'm trying to make points with Dad, so I decided I'd clean my room. It took me longer than I expected."

"You always have some dumb excuse."

Michelle looked closely at her friend. "Boy, are you cranky. Are you sick or something?"

Dana glanced at her parents. "I'm just nervous," she said almost in a whisper. "Did you feel that quake this morning?"

"That was nothing. Stop worrying."

"Did you have any damage at your house yesterday?" Mr. Chang asked.

"No, but the radio report was wrong when it said there was only minor damage in Santa Reyes."

"Oh?" he said. "I was under the impression there was no serious damage."

"Well, believe me, I saw some." She looked at Dana. "That's why I wound up at the hospital last night."

Mr. Chang had started to get up, but at her words, he sat back down. "What happened?"

Michelle told them the story, rather enjoying the limelight. At first she embellished parts, exaggerating Emilio's agonizing moans. But as she remembered how the boy had looked, her voice lowered almost to a whisper and her throat tightened. "Emilio kept hanging onto me. Kept calling me 'On–hell.'" Michelle gave the Changs a sheepish smile. "I guess he thought I was an angel or something."

"Have they lived here long?" Mr. Chang asked.

"One of the neighborhood men said they'd come from Los Angeles. I know they must not have any money. I mean, you should have seen the place where they lived."

"So, are they going to be okay?" Dana asked.

"I don't know. Mr. Garcia had two heart attacks. Emilio may even lose his leg. I might go over and check on them," she said, more for the Changs' benefit than because she really intended to go.

Mrs. Chang looked at her husband. "Martin, you know, I think this would make a great feature story."

"You're right," he said. "Fluke accident . . . the only casualty in the earthquake . . . the homeless . . . small boy may lose a leg . . . local girl a hero. It's got everything." He turned back to Michelle. "How about going with me later today to interview the boy and his grandfather, maybe take some pictures of you with them."

"Oh, I don't know about that, Mr. Chang," Michelle said quickly. "I'm no hero. I just happened to be in the right place at the right time."

"Don't be so modest, Michelle. Go home and change while I run out to make arrangements and get permission from Mr. Garcia. Meet me back here in a few hours. Wear something blue—it photographs well."

"Can I come too?" Dana asked.

"Yes, but you'll have to stay in the waiting room."

As Michelle was leaving, Mr. Chang called out, "I just thought of a title for the story: 'The Angel of Santa Reyes.'"

Five

DRAWING in a deep breath, Michelle reluctantly followed Mr. Chang and Dana to the children's wing of the hospital. Her stomach felt as shaky as that morning's earthquake.

She wiped her sweaty hands on her skirt and looked around. Emilio had been transferred from the critical care unit to the children's wing, which Michelle hoped would be less frightening for the boy. It wasn't anything like the section where her mother had been. The walls were sunny yellow, with pictures of clowns and little animals. In a room across the hall she saw balloons on the ceiling. A huge teddy bear sat on a chair. The place even smelled different, not so . . . mediciney. But Michelle wondered whether that was just her imagination.

Dana took a seat in the waiting area and

began to thumb through a magazine while Michelle and Mr. Chang went to the nurses' station. Mr. Chang explained the purpose of their visit and slid a signed release form from Mr. Garcia across the counter. The form granted permission for the interview. He also explained that the visit had been cleared with the hospital's public relations department and Dr. De Berg.

A nurse whose name tag said "Mrs. Davilo" made a quick call to verify the information, then motioned for Mr. Chang and Michelle to follow her.

At Emilio's door, Michelle hung back, a little afraid of seeing the boy. What if he looked really bad? What if they'd told him he might lose a leg? After inhaling slowly to gain control of her feelings, she finally followed the nurse into the room.

"Emilio, you have visitors," Mrs. Davilo said. "Do you feel like talking for a few minutes?"

The boy seemed dazed and his eyes looked frightened. His leg, covered with a bandage from below his knee to his toes, was raised on a pillow.

"Maybe he doesn't speak English," Michelle whispered.

The nurse stepped aside. Emilio saw

Michelle and his face lit up. Then his expression changed to bewilderment. "I thought you were a dream," he said, without any accent at all.

Michelle figured he must have used the Spanish word for angel when he was half out of his head with pain. He was definitely not born in a foreign country. She moved closer to the bed. "No, I'm real. My name is Michelle."

"She found you and your grandpa," Mr. Chang told him. "You called her 'On-hell'— an angel."

"I did not!" Emilio said stubbornly. "An angel . . . that's dumb." He glared at them. "I want to see Gramps. Nobody'll let me see him."

"Emilio, I've told you a dozen times," the nurse said. "You and your grandfather can visit each other when you're both feeling better."

"Gramps is going to die, isn't he?" Emilio angrily brushed tears away. "That's why you won't let me see him."

The nurse turned to Mr. Chang. "He's upset. Maybe we'd better not do the interview now."

Mr. Chang took charge. "Emilio, I'm from the newspaper. We'd like to do a story about you and Michelle and your grandpa."

Outside, a car backfired and startled the boy. He ducked and covered his head with a trembling hand.

"It's okay," Michelle said. "You're safe here." She didn't blame him for being spooked. If a wall had fallen on her, she'd be nervous too.

"I'm not scared." Emilio's lower jaw stuck out as if daring her to challenge him. "I just don't like this dumb ol' place."

You and me both, kid, thought Michelle.

Mr. Chang pulled up a chair for her, then got out his camera, talking all the while to put the boy at ease. "Why don't you tell us a little about yourself? How old are you?"

"I'm practically seven. After our house burned up in Los Angeles, Gramps and I lived in a lot of places. Then we came here. He's a gardener and can make anything grow. I help." Emilio looked down at his leg. "Gramps needs me."

"Where are your mom and dad?" Michelle asked.

"They're dead," he said in a flat voice. "It's just Gramps and me." Emilio sank back against the pillow.

"He's tired," Mrs. Davilo said. "Take a picture; then you'd better leave."

Mr. Chang took several shots of Michelle sitting beside the bed. Then he took a couple that included the nurse.

As Michelle got up to leave, Emilio asked in an offhand way, as if he didn't really care, "You coming back?" He eyed her warily, waiting for her answer. When she hesitated, he quickly added, "It doesn't matter. I don't want no visitors poking around, asking questions, anyways."

Michelle knew that wasn't true. "No, no . . . I do want to visit. It's just that it might not be right away. I don't know how easily I can get permission. Okay?"

"Okay." Emilio sighed and closed his eyes.

They quietly left the room. At the door, Michelle turned back to look at the boy. A wave of guilt washed over her. She'd been complaining about not seeing as much of her father as she'd like, but at least she had a father. Emilio had no mother or father. Even his grandfather might die. She had a nice home; Emilio was living in a condemned building. She couldn't help admiring the kid. He was obviously scared to death, yet trying to put up a big front. Little kids ought to be able to act like little kids.

Michelle and Mr. Chang headed to where

Dana was waiting.

She looked up from her magazine. "How'd it go? Will he be okay?"

"I guess, but he's scared," said Michelle. "He asked if I'd come back." She groaned. "I can't believe I said yes."

"Michelle, I still need more background information for the story," Mr. Chang said. "I'll see if this is a good time for you to talk to Mr. Garcia."

She wanted to just get out, but Emilio's little face swam into her mind. She knew she was a link to his grandfather. "I guess I can do that."

"You girls stay right here. I'll go see if I can get the green light for you."

Michelle slumped onto a chair. "I wish your dad hadn't come up with this story idea."

Dana gave her a long look. "I know why you hate the hospital. And why you don't want to be a volunteer. When we came in you looked like you were being led to the electric chair. You've never said so, but it's because your mom died here, isn't it?"

Michelle avoided her friend's eyes. "I just don't want to remember those bad times."

"But maybe it's like getting back on a horse after you've fallen. The more times you do it, the easier it gets."

"Maybe," Michelle conceded. But I still don't like—"

Dana grabbed her wrist. "Look!" she whispered. "It's Travis Knight. I could faint! Does my hair look all right?"

"You look fine," Michelle whispered back. She automatically pushed her own hair back and sat up straighter.

Travis was a year ahead of them in school and already had his own car.

"Hi, Travis," Dana said quickly. "We heard you worked here. Do you think the hospital could use more volunteers? Michelle and I were talking about joining the program."

"We can always use more juniors," Travis said. "We're short-handed in the summer. So many kids leave town because of the heat."

"Actually, Dana's the one who's been talking about volunteering," Michelle said quickly. "Myself, I'm really not interested."

"Not everybody's cut out for it," Travis said. "I probably wouldn't have gotten into it if my dad weren't a doctor."

"Michelle's dad is Dr. De Berg," Dana said. "He's been trying to get her to join."

Travis turned to Michelle. "I didn't realize Dr. De Berg was related to you," he said. "He sure is popular. Whenever somebody needs a doctor in an emergency, they always call Dr. De."

"And the emergencies usually happen at night or when we have plans," Michelle said disgustedly. She knew she sounded like a brat and wished she'd kept quiet.

Instead, Travis nodded sympathetically. "It's rough having a doctor in the family. My dad's an anesthesiologist. I think he's missed half of my birthday parties and a lot of my Little League games. That's one reason I joined the volunteers. I figured I'd see him more often."

Dana gave her an I-told-you-so look. "I told Michelle exactly the same thing," she said.

"And do you see him more often?" Michelle asked.

Travis grinned. "Not much." He saw a nurse coming toward them. "I'd better get to work. Nice talking to you both."

When he was out of earshot, Dana pretended to faint and flopped back on her chair. "He's gorgeous. I never could resist tall blond guys with blue eyes you could die for. And I told you the volunteers weren't nerds. I don't care if you join or not. I am."

"Travis's dad would have to anesthetize me to get me to join," Michelle said.

When Mr. Chang returned, he motioned for Michelle to follow him. "I got permission for you to talk to Mr. Garcia for a few minutes."

On the way to the east wing, he told her what questions to ask and handed her a mini-tape recorder.

Reluctantly she took it. "I really hate this," she said. "I've never interviewed anybody. Can't you do it?"

"No," he said. "The old man is more interested in seeing you than me. Just get some background on him. Ask about the parents. You'll do fine." He picked up the phone beside the door to the critical care unit, gave Michelle's name, and said she had permission to see Mr. Garcia.

There were eight beds in the room, but only two were filled. Mr. Garcia was hooked up to oxygen and a heart monitor. His breathing was no longer labored, and Michelle thought his color was better than it had been the night before.

"Mr. Garcia?" she whispered.

At the sound of her voice, he looked up and smiled weakly. "Good. Good. I wanted to thank you for saving my boy." He spoke English well with only a slight accent.

"I didn't do anything much," she protested.

"Ah, I know different. Have you seen my Emilio?"

"Yes, just a few minutes ago. He seems to be doing okay. He's more worried about you."

"We should never have left L.A. It is my fault."

Michelle switched on the recorder. "Would you mind telling me a little about you and Emilio?"

He nodded. "For the paper, yes?"

"Right. Do you have any other family?" she asked, trying to think of a diplomatic way of finding out about Emilio's parents.

"Only some cousins in Mexico. I left there years ago and I have lost track of them. My son and his wife were killed in a hit-and-run accident. My boy went to college," he said proudly. "He was a landscape artist. Then, on their way to work one day, their truck was—" His voice broke and he stopped for a moment. "They were both killed."

"I'm so sorry." Michelle didn't know what else to say.

"Our house . . . well, not long after that, it was destroyed by a fire. We began to live on the streets." Mr. Garcia sounded ashamed.

"Lots of people are having a hard time

making it these days," Michelle said.

"I thought if we came out to a resort town like Palm Grove, I could get work as a gardener, but . . ." His voice trailed off. "What will I do? Where will we go?" he said as if he'd forgotten she were there. "No insurance. No money."

"Don't you qualify for some kind of government assistance?" Michelle asked. She was familiar with some of the government programs that helped provide health care for the elderly or needy. Edith was always complaining about the paperwork.

"Yes, but I don't know about Emilio. I am sorry. These things are not your worry. What else do you want to know?"

They talked a little longer, but Michelle could see that Mr. Garcia was getting tired. "I'd better let you rest. Is there anything I can do for you?"

"I know this is much to ask, but if it is safe to go inside our building, will you bring something of Emilio's? It is a box with his treasures. It is all he has of his own. It would mean so much to him."

Michelle most definitely didn't want to go into that building again. As she struggled with what to say, Mr. Garcia waved a hand and said, "No, never mind.

That is too much to ask."

"It's just that I don't think my dad would let me," Michelle said, feeling relief wash over her. "He was upset with me for being in that part of town."

Mr. Garcia gave a little laugh. "I did not realize. It is so much better than the neighborhood we came from. No, you must not disobey your father." He smiled. "Emilio thought you were an angel. I think maybe he was right."

"My dad would give you an argument about that," Michelle said. She gave Mr. Garcia a little wave and left, glad to be out of that room. But as she walked back to the waiting room, she couldn't keep her mind off Emilio. Poor little kid. What had happened to him just wasn't fair.

Dana and her dad were waiting for her. She handed Mr. Chang the recorder. "Can we go now?"

When they stepped out of the hospital, Michelle greedily gulped at the air. "I hope I never, *ever* have to go back in there."

"But I thought you were planning to check in on the boy later," Dana said.

"I've changed my mind. Emilio himself said he didn't want people poking around. Mr. Chang, you can tell Emilio about his grandfather. I don't need to be there. I mean, it's not like the Garcias are my responsibility."

"Maybe not," Mr. Chang said softly. "But you probably saved their lives. We have an old Chinese saying about that. If you save a person's life, you are responsible for him for the rest of his life."

"Yeah, well, that sounds great, but no way am I going to be responsible for the Garcias for the rest of their lives. No way."

Six

WITH Mookie in her lap, Michelle curled up on her father's leather recliner to watch the Friday night horror movie. But she couldn't concentrate because Emilio's face kept getting in the way.

Stop thinking about him, she told herself. She settled back in the recliner and closed her eyes . . .

It was difficult to even see the child. He was almost covered by concrete rubble. Blood seeped from his forehead and arm. One leg was at an odd angle and a broken bone was poking through the skin. She shook her head, trying to push the memories away.

He opened his eyes, looked up for a second, then whispered something that sounded like, "On-hell."

"Michelle?"

She jerked up, startled by her father's voice.

"Sorry I woke you up, honey."

"I wasn't asleep," she said. "Just thinking."

He loosened his tie and stretched out on the couch with his hands behind his head. "I finally got caught up enough that I don't have to go to the hospital tomorrow. How about getting up early and heading for the beach?"

"Sure," she said absently.

"That's what I like. Enthusiasm." Dr. De Berg looked at his daughter closely. "How did your interviews go today? Martin Chang said he was doing a feature story about you and the Garcias."

"It went okay."

"I checked on both Garcias today. They're doing as well as can be expected."

"Emilio puts up a brave front, but I think he feels lost and afraid. His grandfather said that it would mean a lot to Emilio if he had his box of treasures. It's in that condemned building. Do you think we could get permission to go back in to get it?"

"I guess I could ask the sheriff to let me look for it. I'll make a call first thing in the morning."

Michelle's face lit up. "Thanks, Dad. And if we can get the box, will you take me to the hospital so I can give it to Emilio personally?"

"Okay, but you'd rather do that than go to the beach?"

"Well, Emilio . . . he's more important. Are you sure you don't mind?"

"No. I can always find plenty to do in the office." Her father furrowed his brows. "But aren't you getting too involved with that boy?"

Michelle didn't understand. One minute he was telling her she wasn't responsible enough. The next he was worried because she *was* being responsible

* * * * *

On the way to the hospital the next day, Michelle read the morning paper for the dozenth time. In bold print the headline said, THE ANGEL OF SANTA REYES. The story was excellent—a real tear-jerker—but a small part of Michelle was disappointed that very little was actually about her. Still, she did think the picture of her and Emilio had turned out well. And Mr. Chang had managed to get in a plea for the homeless.

Michelle set the paper aside and pulled the rubber band off Emilio's battered shoe box. It had taken a few phone calls, but her father had persuaded someone from the sheriff's department to retrieve the box from the condemned building. They had picked it up on the way to the hospital.

Carefully, Michelle checked the items inside. There were so few: a wedding picture of a man and a woman—probably Emilio's parents, she guessed—along with a grass-stained baseball, a handful of baseball cards, several sea shells, and a miniature red Lamborghini. She thought of all the things so important to her. Books and CDs and tapes. Her computer and all the video games. The porcelain and crystal animals. The diary she no longer wrote in, but would hate to lose . . . so many things. Emilio's pitifully small box of treasures made her want to cry.

Her father stopped the car in front of the hospital entrance. "I'll be in my office. Stop by when you're through."

As Michelle stepped out of the car, a blast of heat hit her. Just past nine-thirty, and it was already over ninety degrees.

With the box and the newspaper for Emilio under her arm, she hurried to the children's wing. When she started into his room, a nurse stopped her.

"You can't go in there until visiting hours," the nurse told her brusquely.

"I just wanted to give him this." Michelle held up the box. "Emilio's grandfather asked me to bring it to him."

"Leave it at the desk and we'll see that he gets it."

"But I want to give it to him myself. I'm Michelle De Berg and my father is chief of—"

"That doesn't give you special privileges. No one can go into this room now."

"But he needs me. If I were family, you'd let me in. Besides, his grandfather sort of asked me to watch out for him."

The nurse sighed impatiently. "I'm sorry, Miss De Berg. You're a doctor's daughter. You ought to know that during the first part of the day, we're too busy. It's disrupting to have visitors wandering in and out."

Even though she knew the nurse was right, Michelle couldn't shake her irritation. She claimed a seat by Emilio's door and idly snapped the rubber band around the shoe box. What if Emilio lost his leg? He'd never be able to chase the baseball again. Even with the finest equipment, doctors might not save his leg. They hadn't been able to save her mother.

"Mama," she whispered, "why did you have to die?"

Only dimly aware of what she was doing, Michelle started walking to the wing of the hospital where her mother had died. The corridor seemed endless. Nurses pushing carts rattled past her, but she didn't notice. She didn't notice anything until she stopped at the private room at the end of the hall. She looked at the door. Tears stung her eyes.

"My dear, would you mind helping me?" said a soft voice from within the room.

Michelle's hand flew to her mouth. *Mama?* A chill ran down her back.

"I hate to bother you, but I can't brush the back of my hair."

Michelle choked back a sob. Instead of her mother lying pale and lifeless on the bed, a smiling woman sat there, holding a brush.

"My husband will be here in a little while to take me home and I want to look nice. The nurses are all busy." The woman smiled again. "I can't believe it—I'm going home."

Hesitantly, Michelle stepped forward.

"After the way I felt ten days ago, I never thought I'd be leaving this hosp—" The woman stopped abruptly, studying Michelle's face. "Are you all right, dear?" she asked gently. "I've been babbling on. Is there anything I can do?"

Michelle shook her head. "No . . . I . . ." Her voice caught. "There's nothing anyone can do."

The woman got up and went to Michelle, put an arm around her, and drew her to a chair. "Believe it or not, I'm a pretty good listener. Is someone in your family in the hospital?"

"No. She—my mom—died. It was a year ago in this room."

"Oh, I'm so sorry. You shouldn't be alone right now."

"I was alone then. My dad's a doctor. He was in surgery when she died." Tears dampened Michelle's cheeks. "I don't know why I'm here. I had to come back and . . ." Her voice trailed off.

"To say a last goodbye?" The woman handed her a tissue. "To put a finish on it?"

Michelle's eyes burned. "I guess that's it."

The woman took her hand and gently squeezed it. "Have you talked about this to anyone?"

"No. It makes my dad sad when he talks about Mom."

"Believe me, I understand," the woman

said. "When I found out I had to have surgery, I couldn't talk to my husband about it. My mother-in-law, bless her, made us sit down and talk." The woman reached up to brush her hair and flinched.

"Are you okay?" Michelle asked.

"I had a mastectomy and the doctor says I have to use this arm." She grinned. "If it didn't hurt so much, I'd belt him with it."

Michelle chuckled, then put down the shoe box and newspaper. "Here, let me help you with your hair," she said. She took the brush, and ran it through the woman's graying curls. "When I was little, I used to love to brush Mom's hair. She'd pay me a whole twenty-five cents for fifteen minutes. I'd have done it for nothing."

The woman grinned. "With inflation, these days you'd get at least a buck."

When Michelle finished, she said, "I guess I'd better go."

"I'm glad you came in, dear. Just remember, lots of people have been in this room and gotten well."

Michelle nodded. "Thanks. And I'm glad you're going home." At the door, she turned back to look at the room. It was just a room.

She headed back to the children's wing. It wasn't quite eleven o'clock, so she sat down to wait. Two junior volunteers brushed past her, then stopped near Emilio's door. They were carrying pots of flowers. Michelle recognized one of the girls. Amber Berenson was pretty, rich, and always giving parties for a clique of friends. Michelle couldn't imagine why Amber would want to be a volunteer.

The two girls were making fun of some boys and didn't notice Michelle. She heard Emilio call, "Hey, nurse?"

"Jeff is such a nerd," Amber said. "Did you see his clothes? Totally weird."

"Water. I can't reach—"

Michelle heard the sound of something bang against the tile floor.

"Hey, somebody! Please help me," Emilio called.

The girls went right on gossiping.

Furious, Michelle hurried over to them. "Are you two deaf or just plain stupid?"

"Hey, who do you think you are?" Amber said hotly.

Ignoring the remark, Michelle pushed past the girls and into Emilio's room. His yellow water pitcher and cup were on the floor. A puddle was slowly spreading and Emilio was trying to climb over the side rails of the bed.

"No!" Michelle said sharply. Then, more calmly, she added, "Here, I'll help you."

She dropped the shoe box and newspaper on the foot of the bed and rang for the nurse. While she waited, she snatched some paper towels and began to mop up the water. Emilio watched silently.

The nurse who answered the call was the same one who'd kept her from seeing Emilio earlier. "I thought I told you—"

"I heard Emilio calling for help and your two volunteers—your Florence Nightingales out there—just ignored him. He would have fallen from his bed if I hadn't barged in."

The nurse glowered at the two girls in the doorway. "Return to the volunteer's room as soon as you deliver those flowers."

"They're probably wilted by now," Michelle muttered.

Emilio spotted the shoe box and squealed. "My box! My box! Did Gramps bring it? Where is he?"

"I brought it," Michelle said. "Your grandpa asked me to bring it to you."

The nurse raised the head of Emilio's bed a little, then handed him the box. He opened it, checking through the items. He sighed contentedly.

"Now that I'm here, is it okay if I stay for

a while?" Michelle asked the nurse.

"I'm sorry, but Emilio is scheduled for X-rays and tests shortly."

Frustrated, Michelle waved at Emilio. "I'll be back to see you later."

Michelle realized that hospitals needed rules, but being the daughter of the chief of staff ought to count for something. She marched to her father's office.

Dr. De Berg looked up from his desk. "What's wrong, honey?"

"Would you please leave word with Emilio's nurse that I can come and go outside of visiting hours? I mean, I'm not going to get in the way or anything, but he can't see his grandpa yet and he doesn't have anybody. The nurses only care about rules."

Michelle expected him to take her side. Instead, her father said practically the same thing as the nurse. "The nurse might be a little gung ho, but she's got a job to do. I can't bend the rules for you. I'm afraid you'll have to abide by them like anyone else."

Telling Michelle she couldn't do something was like waving a red flag in her face. She'd have to figure out some way to help Emilio.

At home later, she hurried to the phone and called the Changs' number. Hearing

Dana's voice, she blurted out, "Okay, let's do it."

"Do what?"

"Sign up to be junior volunteers. Monday morning."

"How come? What changed your mind?"

"Emilio. If I'm at the hospital, I can keep an eye on him." Michelle told Dana what had happened. "Let's see them keep me out of his room if I'm a volunteer."

"You're sure caught up with this kid. I thought you didn't want to take any responsibility for the Garcias."

"So I changed my mind. I just want to see that they're okay, that's all."

Michelle didn't really understand why she felt so strongly about Emilio and his grandfather. Maybe it had to do with what Mr. Chang had said about saving someone's life—that you were responsible.

Seven

"I don't know how I'm going to remember all that stuff we learned in orientation," Dana said as she selected a ham and cheese sandwich in the hospital cafeteria. She and Michelle had been lucky to get into a class on Tuesday. "And we still have a lot of training to get through."

"I don't see why we have to know all that junk," Michelle said. She put a piece of strawberry pie on her tray and headed for an empty table near the back of the cafeteria.

"I wish they'd let us work as a team," Dana said.

"Yeah, and why can't we choose where we work? I mean, the only reason I volunteered was so I could keep an eye on Emilio."

"I'm scared I'll do something wrong," Dana said.

"Me too. My dad gave me a big speech about being responsible and following the rules. If I do a good job I think he'll let me go to Hawaii."

"So what about the little kid, anyway?"

"Unless his leg gets infected, he should be out of here soon. I have to try to see him today."

"Don't forget about us in the meantime," Dana said. "What if someone has a heart attack while we're in a room? What if there's another earthquake? The 'Big One'?"

"You were so anxious to volunteer. You don't want to back out, do you?"

"No, but it's going to be harder than I thought."

"Dana, I've been thinking. I'll bet Emilio would like my electronic games. I'm going to bring some from home."

"Mrs. Gordon said we weren't supposed to get involved with the patients, you know."

"Yes, but that doesn't mean we have to be like those two," Michelle said. She nodded toward Amber Berenson and the other girl who had been outside Emilio's room. "Believe me, they don't get involved."

"That girl with Amber is Kathy Williams," Dana said. "I didn't know she was in the program."

As the girls came toward them, Dana waved and called out, "Hi, Kathy." And before Michelle realized what Dana was doing, she added, "Come sit with us."

Kathy started forward, then stopped when she recognized Michelle. Her smile faded. "Hi, Dana. What are you doing here?"

"Michelle and I just got out of the volunteer orientation class." She looked from Kathy to Amber and said, "Hi, Amber. Everybody knows who you are, but we've never met. I'm Dana Chang and this is my friend, Michelle De Berg."

"Your friend with the angel wings got us into trouble," Amber said. She turned disdainful eyes on Michelle. "Just because you made the front page of the paper and your dad's chief of staff, Goldilocks, don't get any ideas about being a big shot around here. My father is on the board of directors."

Michelle gritted her teeth to keep from answering back. Amber had drawn a line in the sand. Michelle knew that if she made one mistake, Amber would do something to get her bounced from the program.

"Come on, Kath," Amber said. "Let's find a table where the air is better."

Kathy gave Dana and Michelle an embarrassed smile and followed Amber to a table across the room.

"What did you do to make Amber so mad?" Dana asked.

"*Me* do something! I told you about it. Emilio was calling for help and those two stood there gossiping. I guess the nurse must have reported them."

"Well, it's sure going to make things unpleasant around here," Dana said sullenly, as if she blamed Michelle.

Michelle didn't know whether to feel hurt or angry. Lately, Dana seemed ready to fight every time she opened her mouth.

For the remainder of lunch they sat in silence. Michelle picked at the strawberry pie. For some reason it no longer seemed very appealing.

* * * * *

"I'm Mrs. Covington, and I'll be training you this afternoon," the senior volunteer explained. "I know this all seems confusing at first, but you'll catch on fast. When you complete the training, you'll be teamed with an experienced junior."

Dana nudged Michelle. "I hope we at least get to run into each other once in a while," she whispered.

"You'll have twelve hours of training with me or one of the other senior volunteers," Mrs. Covington went on. "We'll start at the information desk."

There were two adult volunteers at the desk, answering phones and giving directions to visitors. Mrs. Covington smiled at them, then took the class to the side and went over some of the rules about filling out forms.

"Everything must be signed for," she explained, "and you need to note the patient's name and room number, who it was delivered by, and who accepted it. And whenever you deliver something, it must be signed for."

Michelle wondered if she had to sign a form to go to the rest room.

"When you complete an errand, check it off," Mrs. Covington continued. "The main thing to remember is that many of the people coming in are upset and worried. Remain calm and courteous and try to be helpful."

When Mrs. Covington finished giving instructions, she gave them each a map of the hospital and took them on a tour.

"What do we do if there's an earthquake?" Dana asked.

"In case of fire or earthquake, use the stairs, not the elevator," Mrs. Covington said. "Do the same thing you'd do at home. Don't run. Duck under something solid, cover your face and head, and hold on to something until the shaking stops. Stay away from windows. Try to stay calm. As soon as the shaking stops, go to the nearest nurses' station or the volunteer room for instructions."

"When do we get to wear a beeper?" Dana asked.

"As soon as you've completed your training."

"And where do we get the turquoise uniforms like the one you're wearing?"

Mrs. Covington smiled. "You can buy them at the auxiliary office."

The day's training ended at three o'clock.

"We still have a couple of hours before we meet your dad," Dana said. "What do you want to do? It's too hot to walk to the mall. Shall we wait in the volunteer room?"

"No," Michelle said emphatically. "I might run into Amber. I'd like to go see how Emilio's doing. Want to come with me?"

Dana's "I guess so" sounded less than enthusiastic.

"We could get a book and take turns

reading to him," Michelle said. "You're really good at that." A little flattery never hurt.

They went to the library room on the second floor, picked out a couple of books, and took them to the children's wing. When they entered Emilio's room, he was watching TV.

"Hi," Michelle said. "I brought my friend Dana to meet you."

Emilio's face brightened for a moment. Then he frowned and said belligerently, "Thanks for the box, but I thought you would visit me sooner."

"I wanted to, but I've been really busy. Guess what, though? I'm going to be working here as a volunteer. I'll be able to see you a lot. You'll get so tired of me popping into your room, you'll probably kick me out." Michelle grinned and pointed to his injured leg. "But not with that one."

"I thought you was mad at me 'cause I knocked my water pitcher on the floor."

"I'd never get mad at you for something like that. It wasn't your fault." She carried a chair to the side of his bed. "How're they treating you?"

"Okay, I guess, but they still won't let me see Gramps."

"I'll bet they will in a day or two. The last

time I saw him he looked much better."

"Will you go find out for sure?" Emilio begged.

"Sure." Michelle handed the book to Dana. "Why don't you start reading to him? I'll be back in a few minutes."

As Michelle stood up to leave, the floor began to shake and Emilio's bed visibly moved.

"Don't go!" he cried. "Don't go!"

Michelle grabbed him and held him tight. "It's okay, Emilio. It's okay."

His small body was trembling. Though the quaking had stopped, he kept looking at the ceiling and walls, as if they were going to come down on him again.

"It's all over," said Michelle. She tried to make a joke out of it. "You've heard of the cookie monster, haven't you?"

His teeth were chattering as he tried to speak. "Y—e—s."

"Well, the earthquake monster had a stomachache." Michelle made a funny face and held her stomach. "He was stomping on the floor and it shook the whole building." She pretended to stomp around the room.

"There ain't no monster and you look pretty dumb."

"I just did that for Dana's benefit,"

Michelle said. "She doesn't like earthquakes."

She glanced at Dana, who seemed frozen to the middle of the floor. If anything, she appeared even more upset than Emilio.

"Hey, Dana, I thought you were going to read Emilio a story," Michelle said brightly, hoping to distract them both. "Emilio, when I get back, you can tell me what I've missed."

Michelle hung around until she saw Dana begin to read. Then she went to the critical care unit, only to be told by the nurse that she couldn't go in. "Mr. Garcia had a bad night. He's asleep."

"Will you give him a message?" asked Michelle, wishing there were more she could do. "His grandson misses him."

What was it about this little boy that drew her, anyway? She hardly knew him. Was it because he tried so hard to be brave? Or was it because he needed her?

Eight

O N Friday, when they had finished their training, Michelle and Dana headed for the volunteer room to get their schedules for the coming week.

Mrs. Gordon, the administrator of the volunteer program, sat at her desk. She looked stern, but her voice sounded friendly.

"Congratulations and welcome to our family of volunteers." She got out a chart. "Which days and shifts are you available to work?"

"We've decided on full days, Monday through Friday," Michelle said. "Is that okay?" The more time she spent in the hospital, the more opportunity she would have to see Emilio. What few visits she had managed during training were all too brief.

"Actually, if you can spend that much time here, it would be wonderful," Mrs. Gordon said. "We're a little short-handed now. But

74

are you sure the Fourth of July holiday on Tuesday is okay with your families?"

Michelle and Dana both nodded. "We're staying in town," said Michelle. "Our families are celebrating the Fourth at the park that night, so we can work the day."

Mrs. Gordon looked at the chart. "Dana, on Monday you'll work with Travis Knight."

Michelle thought Dana would squeal out loud, but she managed to say quietly, "That'll be fine."

"Michelle, you'll team with Amber Berenson."

Now it was Michelle who wanted to squeal, but for an entirely different reason. She bit her lip. "I thought Amber worked with Kathy Williams."

"She usually does, but Kathy's going out of town."

"Isn't there anybody else? Can I trade with someone?"

"I'm afraid not." Mrs. Gordon gave Michelle a close look. "Is there a problem between you and Amber?"

"No," she said quickly.

"Good, because we can't have any friction between the volunteers. The patients' welfare is the only thing you should have on your mind."

"Right," Michelle said. "We'll be here by eight o'clock. We bought uniforms last night."

Mrs. Gordon eyed Michelle critically. "I'll see you girls Monday. And remember, we're a team around here."

*   *   *   *   *

Travis was already in the volunteer office on Monday when Michelle and Dana arrived at quarter to eight.

"Hi, Travis, I'm your partner today," Dana said shyly. A blush raced up her neck and settled over her face.

"Great," he answered as he pinned on his name tag. "Who are you teamed with?" he asked Michelle.

"Amber Berenson." She thought his lips quivered just a little, as if he were trying to conceal a smile.

By the time Amber sauntered in at eight-fifteen, only Michelle and Mrs. Gordon were left in the room. The other volunteers had already left on assignments.

"Sorry I'm late," Amber said to Mrs. Gordon. When she realized that Michelle was the only volunteer left in the room, her lips tightened. For a moment Michelle thought Amber would refuse to work with her. Instead, she offered a sugar-coated smile, but said nothing.

When Amber put on her beeper, Michelle asked Mrs. Gordon, "Don't I get one too?"

"We're having several serviced. You'll get one in a few days." She turned to Amber. "You two can give out the complimentary morning newspapers."

Neither girl spoke as they went to the information desk to get a stack of papers. They each took half and began to distribute them.

Michelle only had a few of her papers left when Amber met her in the hall. "I just got a call on my beeper," Amber said. "You're supposed to pick up some medicine at the pharmacy. It's for room 218. I'll finish with the papers and meet you in the library room."

Michelle didn't say anything, but it struck her that Amber sounded friendlier. After their confrontation in the cafeteria, Michelle had expected Amber to be sarcastic—even nasty.

She picked up the medicine and delivered it to the south wing. When she got to the library room, Amber was out of breath, as if she'd been running. "You're supposed to get some X-rays from the radiology lab. Hurry, Michelle. They're in a big rush. Meet me in the lounge when you're through."

The elevators were full, so Michelle ran down the stairs, picked up the X-rays, and hurried back to the south wing. She started to give them to the nurse at the station, then remembered to get confirmation that they were the correct ones.

Amber sent her to radiology again, to the front desk, to the lab, back to the pharmacy. Starting to get tired, she walked slowly back to the lounge where she found Amber watching TV and fanning herself with a magazine.

"Whew," Amber said. "I just had to sit down a minute."

Michelle started to plop on the couch when Amber said, "Whoops. I almost forgot. You need to get a wheelchair from downstairs and take it to Room 217."

"I thought we were supposed to do some of these things together," Michelle said.

"I know, but we're just too busy. When you're through, come back here. If I'm on an errand, just wait for me."

Michelle found the wheelchair in the lobby and took it Room 217. It was empty. She went to the nurses' station, then looked up and down the hall for someone to ask what she should do. Finally a nurse's aide came out of the room across from 217, where Michelle had delivered the medicine earlier.

The aide motioned for her to bring the wheelchair. "What took you so long?" Her voice was decidedly irritated.

"I had the wrong room number, and I couldn't find—"

"This isn't the right chair," the aide said, breaking in. "I distinctly asked for an oversized chair."

"I'm sorry, I didn't know."

A cranky voice came from the room. "What's the hold up? I want to go home."

"It'll be just a few minutes, Mrs. Gillespie." The aide turned back to Michelle. "Hurry and get that larger chair."

I'm doing the best I can, Michelle thought. *I'm running my legs off and I get yelled at.*

She was almost breathless by the time she got the oversized chair back upstairs. The aide was making a last-minute check of the closet and drawers. Mrs. Gillespie, wearing a flowered robe, sat on the edge of the bed. She looked as if she weighed at least 250 pounds. Michelle groaned, wondering how she would manage to push the chair with the woman in it.

The nurse's aide settled the woman in the chair with a small bag, a potted plant in her lap, and a cane across the chair arms.

"I may need some help," Michelle said.

The aide unlocked the brakes. "I'll come down with you."

Mrs. Gillespie complained steadily about the food, the doctors, and the nurses' incompetence. "I don't feel any better than when I checked in here a week ago."

At the desk, the aide asked for a transporter to help get the patient into a waiting taxi. When the woman was finally settled inside, the aide waved and called out a hearty goodbye. "You stay healthy now, Mrs. Gillespie," she said.

Michelle had never heard any wish sound so heartfelt. "What was she in here for?" she asked.

"She comes into emergency every few months. She's obese, has diabetes and extremely high blood pressure, but refuses to follow the doctor's orders or watch her diet."

Michelle glanced at her watch. It was almost eleven. "Well, thanks for helping me. I'd better get back now."

At the desk, she signed her name to show

that she'd completed her assignment, then hurried back up to the lounge. Amber wasn't there, so she went down to the cafeteria. By the time she got there, she felt too hot and tired to eat much. All she got was some peach yogurt.

She spotted Dana and Travis at a table and joined them. "Hi," she said flopping in a chair. "I'm totally beat."

"How come?" Travis said. "We hardly had anything to do this morning."

"I guess Amber and I got all the calls. I haven't stopped running all morning."

"That's weird," Dana said. "I saw Amber reading a magazine in the library, and later we saw her in the lounge watching TV."

"I wondered why she was acting so nice," Michelle said, starting to boil. "I've been had by dear Amber. She sat around while she had me running all the over the hospital, and she was giving me wrong directions." She rubbed her sore shoulders. "I hope I never have to push a crabby old lady in an oversized wheelchair ever again."

Travis grinned. "Mrs. Gillespie, I'll bet. Nobody likes to go to her room."

Michelle saw Amber at the back of the cafeteria. "Excuse me," she said to Dana and Travis. "I have something to take care of."

She marched to Amber's table. With her hands on her hips, she stared at the girl for a long moment.

"Oh, hi," Amber said brightly. "Sorry I couldn't wait for you any long—"

"You think you've been real cute, don't you? I'm warning you, don't try any more of your cheap tricks."

"I don't know what you're talking about," Amber said, her eyes wide and innocent.

"I know what you were doing and I don't like it. This afternoon, we'll either go together or we'll take turns answering the calls."

"Oh, well, Michelle, I'm afraid you're on your own the rest of the day. I just developed a terrible headache." Amber pressed her temple. "I'm going to have to go home."

"I don't get you, Amber. You're a lousy volunteer, so why do it? What do you get out of it?"

Amber looked at her watch and stood. "You'd better report back." She was all mock sweetness now. "You don't want to be late." She brushed past Michelle, deliberately bumping her arm.

Michelle seethed. She knew she was in for a battle eventually. She also knew that when it came, she would be ready.

Nine

THE next day, Michelle was teamed with a senior volunteer named Mr. Woodruff, who everybody affectionately called "Woody." Woody was in his seventies, but he moved and talked like a much younger man.

They made up beds and took medical records to various departments. Woody was a wealth of information. Once, on a trip to the lab to carry urine, he showed her where to find gloves and explained, "We have to wear gloves whenever we carry blood or urine, to prevent contamination and possible infection." There were containers of the thin rubber gloves in every room and in the halls.

Later, when the calls had dropped off, Michelle asked if they could stop by the children's wing. "As long as we're not busy, is it okay if I go see a friend?"

"Don't see why not," Woody said. "I like to spend any extra time—" His beeper went off before he could finish. "Hold it. Somebody wants us."

They had two errands—one to the pharmacy, the other to the gift shop. "Pharmacy needs a pick-up on some medication," said Woody. "Will you take that one? It'll save these old legs."

As Michelle hurried to the pharmacy, she thought about the games she'd brought for Emilio. He was going to love them. She picked up the medicine for delivery and ran up the stairs to the second floor. The nurse wasn't at the station. She waited impatiently until she saw a man in a wheelchair in the doorway of the room. Anxious to get going, she took the prescription to him.

"Here's your medicine," Michelle said, handing him the medication. He seemed about to start up a conversation, so she said, "Have a nice day," and took off.

She made a quick detour to pick up the games, then hummed aloud on her way to Emilio's room. A sign on the door stopped her cold: "ISOLATION." A weight settled in Michelle's stomach. *Please let him be all right.*

She hurried to the station. "Where's Mrs.

Davila?" she asked the nurse on duty.

"It's her day off. Can I help you?"

"What does it mean when there's an isolation sign on a door?"

"It means that the patient either has a contagious disease or is too ill for anyone but doctors, nurses, and close family to see him."

"What about Emilio Garcia? What's wrong with him?" Michelle's voice grew shrill. "He was doing just fine."

"He's a very sick boy."

"Can I just say hello to him?" Michelle asked.

"I'm sorry, but no," said the nurse. She gave Michelle a sympathetic look. "Doctor's orders."

The rest of the day was a blur. All Michelle could think about was Emilio. Her dad had told her that if Emilio's leg got infected he could lose it. The thought made her stomach knot. Emilio was mentally tough, but could he handle losing his leg?

* * * * *

That evening, on the way to the park for Fourth of July festivities, Michelle did little more than stare out the car window.

"You're awfully quiet," her father said. "What's wrong?"

"Guess I'm just tired."

"Rough day?" he asked.

"It's Emilio," said Michelle. "He's in isolation. They wouldn't let me see him. Dad, I think his leg is infected."

"I was afraid of that. The artery was compromised. But, honey, they're doing everything they can for the boy."

"I know, but . . . isn't there *some* way I could get in to visit him?"

"We'll see. For right now, though, try to put him out of your mind and have a good time. We haven't been on a picnic since—"

"Since Mom died," Michelle finished quietly.

"That's why you're so worried about Emilio, isn't it? Because of Mom?"

"Why wouldn't I be? You're a doctor and even you couldn't save her."

Her father looked as if he had been kicked in the stomach.

"I'm sorry, Dad, but what good are doctors and hospitals if they can't save people?"

"Honey, we do the best we can. Nobody feels any worse than a doctor does when he loses a patient." His voice was choked. "Especially when it's someone you love."

Michelle reached out and touched his hand. "I went to the room where Mom . . ." Tears blurred her eyes. "I didn't think I could do it."

"Oh, sweetheart, I've been stupid. That's why you didn't want to be a volunteer. That's why you always made an excuse not to come to the hospital. It's such a part of me, I just didn't think how it might affect you. Look, if this volunteer thing is too much for you—"

"No, it's okay, Dad. There was a lady in the room. She reminded me that since the time Mom died, lots of people have stayed in the same room and gotten well again. I'm . . . it really is okay now."

They had reached the parking area. Before he opened the door, Michelle's father reached out and squeezed her hand. "Let's try to have fun tonight. We've hardly had any time together since you started working at the hospital."

That was a switch, Michelle thought. Always before, that was *her* complaint.

Santa Reyes Park, located beside a man-made lake, was cooler than the rest of the town. Palm trees rustled in the slight breeze.

"Over here," Mr. Chang called out. Mrs.

Chang and Dana were already laying out food. Michelle's dad carried the big picnic basket Mrs. Peterson had packed and set it on the table.

"We were lucky to get such a good spot," Mrs. Chang said. "We'll have a good view of the fireworks display. Hope we're not too near the bandstand."

"You may not be able to hear the music over my growling stomach," Michelle's father said. "I'm starving."

Everyone began loading up paper plates with potato salad and fried chicken. "I have great news for you, Michelle," Mr. Chang said. "You won't believe the response we've had from the 'Angel of Santa Reyes' story. Donations are pouring in for the Garcias."

"We set up a special 'Angel' fund," Mrs. Chang added. "Martin wants to do a follow-up story about the community's response."

"Maybe we could include a picture of you presenting a check to the Garcias," Mr. Chang said.

"That sounds great," said Michelle. "Mr. Garcia is worried about what he's going to do when he's released from the hospital. He and Emilio sure can't go back to that condemned building."

"There are lots of other homeless people

around," Dana muttered. "I don't know why the Garcias are so special."

"You're right, honey," Dana's father said. "But every so often a story comes along that touches people. We can't help everybody in the world, but I guess if we help someone, that's better than noth—"

"Dad," Dana said, breaking in, "as soon as we eat, will you take me for a canoe ride?"

Mr. Chang seemed surprised at the interruption, but he didn't comment on it. "A canoe ride sounds great. How about you, Michelle?" he asked.

"Thanks, but I want to talk to Dad."

"Okay, but it can't be for long," her father said. "I promised to man the first-aid booth for an hour. But I should be back in time for the fireworks." He took a bite of watermelon. "These seedless melons aren't any fun. Michelle, remember when we used to have seed-spitting contests?"

"I'm too old for that stuff now," Michelle said. "I have more serious things to think about."

"Ever since you found that kid Emilio, you're no fun at all," Dana said. "Come on, Dad, let's go canoeing. Mom, are you coming?"

"I'll pass," Mrs. Chang said. "I want to

read some of my mystery story before dark. You be careful now, Dana. Wear a life jacket!"

When Dana and Mr. Chang left, Michelle's father moved over beside her. "What did you want to talk about?"

"It's about the Garcias. Even if he doesn't lose that leg, Emilio's going to need lots of therapy. And it's going to cost a lot, isn't it?"

"Yes. I'm afraid those donations won't cover all their expenses. I've got someone checking into the possibility of getting him some government assistance. The trouble is, there are no guarantees he'll get everything he needs."

Michelle had been looking at the park's manicured lawn and flower gardens. "Mr. Garcia's a gardener. When he's better, how about if we hire him to do our yard and the grounds around your office?"

"Well . . . I haven't had a regular gardener for some time."

"Right," Michelle said with rising excitement. "And since the Garcias have no place to live, they could stay at our house. We have that extra guest room and bath. Nobody's used it in ages."

"Michelle, I'm not sure it's a good idea to take them in," her father said. "I can see hiring Mr. Garcia to work around the place, but having him and the boy stay with us could present problems. When Emilio gets out of the hospital, who's going to help him? I also don't think Mrs. Peterson would look too kindly on the extra laundry and cleaning."

"I can learn how to help Emilio with therapy. And I could help out more around the house."

"I'm sure you would, too—for about a week. Then you'd find some excuse to get out of it. You don't have a very good track record for staying with things."

"People can change, you know."

"I'll have to give it a lot of thought," he said. "Besides, for all you know, the Garcias may not want to stay with us. They may consider it charity."

"You will think about it, though?" Michelle asked.

"Yes." Her father looked at his watch. "But not now. I have work to do."

After her father left, Mrs. Chang put down her paperback and looked at Michelle for a long time. The band had started warming up, filling the air with discordant sounds.

"What's up?" Michelle said over the noise.

"Why are you looking at me like that?"

"I'm sorry, dear. I was just thinking. You're really caught up with the Garcias, aren't you?"

Michelle sighed. "I don't know why everybody is on my case about them. What's the big deal?"

"No big deal," Mrs. Chang said. "It's just a matter of balance."

"I don't know what you mean," Michelle said.

"I've noticed some tension between you and Dana." Mrs. Chang smiled ruefully. "Martin and I even have the use of the phone these days. You two are usually on it."

"We've both been busy with volunteering and all."

"Oh, I suspect it's more than that, Michelle."

"You're talking about the Garcias," Michelle said. She frowned. "Dana doesn't understand."

"Maybe that's because you don't have time for her anymore," Mrs. Chang said quietly. "I'm sure you don't mean to shut her out, Michelle, but she's hurt."

Michelle didn't say anything for a bit. "I guess I have been pretty involved. But Dana's my best friend. I thought she would realize this is just temporary—that as soon as Emilio is better, I won't be worrying about him all the time."

"Yes, but now you're talking about getting them to live with you. That doesn't seem very temporary."

Michelle gave a little laugh. "I kind of sound like my dad, don't I? That's the way he is about his patients and the hospital."

"There is a similarity."

"It's weird, Mrs. Chang. I've been griping about that for ages. And here I am doing the same thing." Michelle sighed. "I guess I do know how Dana feels."

She went over to Mrs. Chang and kissed her on the cheek. "Thanks. I wouldn't want to lose Dana's friendship for anything in the world."

They both stopped talking to listen to a rousing version of "Seventy-Six Trombones." When Michelle saw Dana and Mr. Chang returning, she hurried toward them.

"How was the canoe ride?" she asked. "Dana, remember the time we tipped over?"

Dana shot her a surprised look, as if she couldn't quite believe that Michelle was interested. Then she grinned. "Which time? All you have to do is look at a canoe and it flops over," she teased.

As they walked back to the picnic table, the two of them lagged behind Mr. Chang. "I keep meaning to ask you," Michelle said, "how do you like teaming with Travis?"

"He's super. And here's something neat—I found out that he only lives about a block from Francine's mobile home park. Oh, speaking of her, she wants me to house-sit and watch her dog next weekend. She's going to a golf tournament in Pebble Beach. Want to come stay with me?"

Michelle hesitated briefly, thinking about Emilio. Then she thought about what Mrs. Chang had said. "Sure, Dana. It'll be fun."

Just then a rocket whined through the air and burst into hundreds of sparkling lights.

"I hope—" Michelle stopped. She was about to say she hoped the fireworks wouldn't frighten Emilio. Instead she said, "I hope Dad gets back here to watch the display."

Sometimes, maybe it was better not to say everything you were thinking about to a friend.

Ten

"IF I'm not on an errand, I'll meet you at eleven o'clock for lunch," Michelle said firmly the next morning.

She and Dana were pinning their name tags to their uniforms. Dana's expression showed mild surprise. Michelle had spent so many of her lunch breaks trying to learn about the Garcias that the girls had rarely eaten together.

After her talk with Mrs. Chang, Michelle decided to work harder at being a better friend. But another part of her mind was on Emilio. What if he were worse this morning?

A voice interrupted her thoughts. "Michelle, I'd like to speak to you," Mrs. Gordon said.

Michelle made a what-did-I-do-now face to Dana and followed Mrs. Gordon into her office.

"Last night we got an irate call," Mrs. Gordon began. "A patient who was released yesterday said he was given the wrong medicine."

"That could be pretty bad," Michelle said, wondering what it had to do with her.

"It's *extremely* serious, and we have safeguards against that happening. I understand you delivered a prescription to Room 253 yesterday."

"I don't remember all the room numbers. But I did make a drop-off to the second floor."

"And when you took it to the nurses' station, did you have a nurse sign for it?"

"I always—" Michelle stopped, remembering that she'd given the medicine directly to the patient. Her face reddened. "Yesterday I didn't," she said in a small voice. "I was in a big hurry. I'm really sorry. Is he okay?"

"Luckily, he realized it wasn't his prescription before he took it. Since no harm was done, we'll forget about this, but I must warn you, we cannot tolerate carelessness."

"I promise I'll be careful," Michelle said. When she came out of the room she let out her breath in a low whistle. She started to walk off when she heard someone call her name.

"Michelle? Uh, for better or worse, you're

teamed with me this morning." It was Kathy Williams. "We're supposed to take the menus around so the patients can fill them out."

Neither spoke as they rode the elevator upstairs.

"When you finish your side of this wing, why don't we meet in the lounge?" Kathy said. When Michelle agreed with a shrug, Kathy looked like she wanted to say something else, but she didn't. Instead, she gave Michelle a tentative half-smile, then quickly looked away.

Before Michelle had even reached the second room, she heard loud complaining and recognized the voice. Already, Mrs. Gillespie was back and giving the nurses and aides a fit.

"How dare you accuse me of smoking! I want to see Dr. De this minute. I don't care if he is in a meeting."

"Dr. De Berg will be here just as soon as he can, Mrs. Gillespie," the aide said as she was leaving.

Michelle forced a smile. "Good morning, Mrs. Gillespie." She smelled the cigarette smoke instantly. "Nice to see you again."

"What do you mean by that?" the woman said with a frown.

"Nothing," Michelle said, taken aback.

"Nothing at all. Here's your menu to fill out." She dropped it on the bedside table.

As she started to hurry out, Mrs. Gillespie said, "Turn on the television to channel four. My favorite soap opera comes on soon."

The remote control was right on the arm of the bed, but Michelle switched on the set. A game show was on.

"Turn it louder. I can't hear it."

Michelle turned up the volume and started to leave.

"Find my glasses," the woman ordered. "That incompetent aide hid them somewhere."

Michelle looked around. "I don't see them anywhere."

"Look for them! Don't just stand there."

Biting her lip to keep from saying something she'd regret, Michelle searched the drawers, looked on the floor, under the bed, in the bathroom—everywhere she could think of. "Maybe they're in your purse," she finally suggested.

"Never mind, I found them myself," Mrs. Gillespie said as she pulled the glasses from under her pillow. "I've never seen a hospital with such poor help."

Then why don't you go to another one?

Michelle said under her breath.

"Before you leave, hand me my box of candy," Mrs. Gillespie ordered. "It's in my drawer under the gown."

Michelle hesitated. She knew a diabetic shouldn't eat a lot of candy.

"Are you deaf, girl?"

By now Michelle was so nervous, her hand shook when she handed the woman the box. It flipped out of her hand, spilling chocolates all over the bed.

"You clumsy fool!" Mrs. Gillespie cried.

"I'm sorry," Michelle said. "Here, let me help—"

"Just get out!" Mrs. Gillespie yelled. "And don't come back."

As Michelle fled, she almost bumped into Amber, who was carrying a florist box.

"Poor Michelle," Amber said mockingly. "Having a bad day?"

"Why don't you just shut up?" Shaking with anger, Michelle pushed past her. Instead of going to the lounge, Michelle hurried to the desk in the children's wing to check on Emilio.

"Mrs. Davila? How's Emilio? Is he any better? I saw the isolation sign on his door yesterday. Please tell me what's wrong with him."

"We don't ordinarily give out a patient's condition except to relatives, but I suppose this is an unusual circumstance. Emilio's leg is infected. His white count is high and he's running a fever."

No . . . Michelle's shoulders slumped. Infection in the leg meant he could lose it. "What's going to happen?" she asked, almost in tears.

"He's on antibiotics. We're doing everything we can."

"Could I just peek in on him?"

"Not now. The doctor's with him."

Michelle walked slowly to the lounge where Kathy was waiting. "I was beginning to think you got lost," Kathy said. "I wanted a chance to talk to you."

Talking was the last thing Michelle wanted to do, but Kathy looked serious. She slumped onto the couch. "Sure."

"I wanted to tell you that I feel awful about the day Amber and I were talking outside that little boy's room. I honestly didn't hear him calling. I don't have any excuse. Amber and I were wrong. I don't blame you for turning us in."

"I was really ticked off at you both, but I didn't report it," Michelle said. "It must have been the nurse. She was—"

Kathy's beeper went off. The volunteer at the desk wanted some medical reports taken to the lab. As they headed for the elevator, Kathy told Michelle that her mother was a nurse in a convalescent home, and her father was a veterinarian. Kathy wanted to go into the medical field and thought that volunteering was a good way to find out if she were suited for the work.

"What about you?" Kathy asked. "Why'd you join?"

"So I could see my dad more often and help Emilio. But now, I think I might even like to learn more about medical careers."

But she wondered—was her dad right? Would she still want that next week? Or next month? Like he'd said, she didn't have a very good track record for sticking with things.

Later, when she checked with her father about taking Mr. Garcia to see Emilio, he said, "Sorry, honey. I talked to Emilio's doctor. The boy's condition is too serious."

Was everything going to turn out like it had with Mom all over again? What was the point of hospitals, and nurses and doctors, if they couldn't save a little boy?

* * * * *

Every morning for the rest of the week, Michelle went to the children's wing to find out about Emilio. And every day there was no change. If only they'd let her in to see him, maybe she could get him to fight.

On Friday, she was teamed with Travis for the first time. He was easy to work with—serious about the job, but fun, too.

Travis got two calls over the beeper, one to the lab, the other to take the patient in 227 down to the desk.

"Room 227. . . that's Mr. Garcia!" Michelle said. "They must be releasing him. Let me take that call, Travis."

Michelle got a wheelchair and hurried to 227. The old man was sitting on the edge of the bed, his shoulders slumped and his head down.

"Mr. Garcia?" Michelle forced a smile. "I guess you're leaving us today, huh?"

Most people seemed eager to get out of the hospital, but he looked around the room as if he hated to leave. He gave a resigned sigh. "Yes. They say I must go."

As Michelle helped him into the wheelchair, she felt him shaking. "Are you sure you're well enough to leave?"

He touched his chest. "The doctor says I am tough and will soon be back to work."

He gave her a twisted smile. "I think there is more work for doctors than for gardeners."

Even when he was very ill, he had never sounded so depressed and hopeless. "I haven't had a chance to tell you, but remember the article about Emilio and me?" asked Michelle. "Well, the Changs set up a fund for you two, and people have started sending money."

"I know," he said. "But I told Mr. Chang that all the money must go for Emilio."

"You can't go back to that condemned building. What will you do? Where will you go?"

"I must stay close by so I can see my Emilio every day." Mr. Garcia's voice broke. "There is a place for me at the homeless shelter here in Palm Grove."

"How is Emilio? They won't let me in to see him because I'm not a relative."

"I have hardly seen him myself. And just now I had to tell him goodbye." Tears clouded the old man's eyes. "He is so very sick." His adam's apple fluttered up and down. "I think he knows now that he may lose his leg."

"He has to fight off the infection." Michelle gently shook Mr. Garcia's shoulders. "We can't let him give up."

Mr. Garcia reached up and touched Michelle's cheek. "I said it before, and I will say it again. You are indeed an angel."

"Hey, that's my job." Michelle forced a smile and pretended to flap her arms as if they were wings. "I'm the Angel of Santa Reyes."

An aide came in to strip the bed. Mr. Garcia took one last look at the room. "It is time to go," he said in a whisper.

Michelle wheeled Mr. Garcia down to the desk. When he finished signing papers, she wheeled him out through the automatic doors into the scorching desert air.

It was crazy. When patients were released, hospital rules said they had to ride in a wheelchair. So, here was Mr. Garcia, riding in a chair through the cool hospital, but immediately faced with the prospect of having to walk in hundred-degree weather to—where?

Angry, Michelle pushed his chair back into the hospital.

"What is wrong?" he asked, looking bewildered.

"You wait right here. I'll be back in a minute." She hurried to her father's office, only to learn from his secretary that he was in yet another meeting.

Michelle dug in her pocket. She only had three quarters and her cafeteria card, worth a dollar. "Sharon, can I borrow ten dollars? I'll pay you back."

The secretary sifted through her purse and handed Michelle a bill. "Are you in trouble or something?"

"No, I just need to help a friend. Thanks."

She dashed back to Mr. Garcia. "I'm calling you a taxi." She handed him the ten dollars. "This ought to cover it."

He smiled. "I think there would be some very surprised faces if I drove up to a homeless shelter in a taxi." He tried to hand back the money. "I will be fine."

Michelle shook her head. "You keep the money, Mr. Garcia. I don't think you should walk too far in this heat. You can catch a bus at the corner and have enough for food tomorrow." She hugged him. "Please take care of yourself. Emilio needs you."

Mr. Garcia got out of the chair, straightened his shoulders, and with a little wave to her, he walked away.

Now she knew where Emilio had gotten his courage and toughness. They were going to make it. They had to.

Eleven

MICHELLE found Travis in the volunteer room. "Travis, Mr. Garcia just left, and I know Emilio must feel terribly alone. I have to see him. Will you cover for me?"

Travis only hesitated briefly. "Okay, but remember that Mrs. Gordon's a stickler for rules."

"I'll take my chances. Thanks, Trav. See you at lunch."

Michelle hurried upstairs, glad now that she didn't have her own beeper yet. Nobody could find her. An aide was at the nurses' station, but her back was to Emilio's door.

Acting as if she were supposed to be there, she slipped into his room. *Oh, Emilio.* He looked so ill. His black hair was wet from sweat and he kept licking his chapped lips.

As Michelle approached the bed, Emilio opened his eyes and blinked, as though they wouldn't quite focus. His eyes, usually so brown and alive, looked faded. He attempted a smile, but the effort was too much and his eyelids fluttered closed again.

Michelle pulled up a chair and took his feverish hand. Now that she was here, she had no idea what to say. Maybe it was stupid to have sneaked in. If she said the wrong thing, she might make Emilio feel even worse. But she had to try, had to share her own strength.

"Emilio," she said softly, "I'm not supposed to be here because I'm not a relative. But I want you to know, I wish you were my little brother."

She poured ice water from his pitcher onto a cloth and wiped his hot forehead. "You have to fight to get well. I know you're tough. You can beat this."

He opened his eyes and she saw the terrible pain in them. "They're gonna—" Tears slid down his cheeks. "They're gonna cut off my leg."

"Not if you can get over the infection." Michelle squeezed his hand. "You have to try. Say it to yourself over and over again— 'infection, you're gone, you're out of here!' See yourself playing baseball and soccer. Imagine yourself skating."

"I don't know how to skate," he said in a pitiful little voice.

"I'll teach you. You get well and we'll do lots of things together. I can help you with your therapy. But you've got to really try."

"I'm so tired. . . ."

"Emilio, you listen to me. I say you're going to get well. I'm an angel, aren't I? So you have to mind me."

The boy rewarded her with a tiny smile.

"I have to go before the nurse catches me, but you remember what I said. You're going to get over the infection. This angel has spoken." Michelle leaned over and kissed his hot little cheek. "You can do it," she whispered. "I'm counting on you."

Michelle managed to leave the room without anyone stopping her, but had to pass Amber in the hall a few seconds later. Amber gave Michelle a look but said nothing. Michelle couldn't tell what the look meant and was too upset about Emilio to think about it. Halfway to the elevator, she had to lean against the wall. Her legs shook from exhaustion. She felt as if every ounce of energy in her body had drained away.

"You okay, Michelle?"

She looked up to see Travis. "I guess so. I'm just tired."

"That's why they tell you not to get involved with patients," he said. "It takes too much out of you."

"Don't lecture me, Trav. I can't help how I feel. That little boy has to get well."

"I'm not lecturing. I've gotten close to patients too. Come on," he said gently. "Let's go to the cafeteria."

Dana, Kathy, and Amber were already there. Travis waved to them. "Save us a seat."

Michelle wanted nothing to do with Amber, but she didn't have the strength to make a scene. She bought a cold drink and joined the others at the long table at the back.

"Well, well, your Highness," Amber said. "So you've decided to eat with the peasants?"

Too tired to rise to the bait, Michelle said, "Hi, every—"

"You'll never in a million years guess what 218 did the other day," Amber said, breaking in.

"What—besides complain?" Kathy asked.

"Well, I took a box of roses, long-stemmed ones, mind you, to Gillespie's room. It was right after you took her the menu," Amber said to Michelle. "I heard her giving you a bad time. Anyway, she asked me to open the box. The card wasn't in an envelope and I couldn't help reading it."

"Sure you couldn't," Travis and Kathy said in unison.

"Do you want to hear what it said, or not?" Amber didn't even wait for an answer. "It's so weird. The note said 'To my Beloved, whose beauty takes men's breath away.'" Amber gave a short burst of laughter. "I mean, really. Can you imagine a guy writing that to that old witch? I'll bet she sent the flowers to herself."

"Maybe her husband sent them," Dana said. "Maybe she still looks beautiful to him."

"She's a widow," Amber said. "Her husband was one of the biggest contributors to the hospital. You know what? I think she wanted people to read the note."

"That's really sad," Dana said. "She must be terribly lonely."

"I can understand why she doesn't have any friends," Amber said. "She's a royal pain. You should have heard the way she laid into Goldilocks here, especially after she spilled bonbons all over the bed." Amber gave Michelle an amused smile. "What did you do? Throw the box at her?"

"Amber, why don't you lay off?" said Travis. "We've all had run-ins with Gillespie."

"Personally, I think she's a hypochondriac."

"She has diabetes and high blood pressure," Travis said. "She never does anything the doctors tell her to do, but she's not a hypochondriac."

"I think she's just unhappy," Michelle said wearily.

"I don't know how you can be so charitable," Amber said. "Not after the way she belittled you."

"Forget it," said Michelle. "Let's change the subject."

"Right," Kathy agreed. "Has anyone been to the new ice rink in the mall?"

"It's great," Travis said. "Why don't we all go tonight? We could make it a party."

"I wish we could," said Dana, "but Michelle and I have to house-sit my grandmother's place this weekend."

Michelle barely listened. All she could think about was Emilio.

She jumped as Travis's beeper went off. They could all hear Mrs. Gordon's grim voice. "Travis, will you please send Miss De Berg to my office? Immediately."

Everyone stared at her.

"She sounded serious," Michelle said. "I wonder what she—oh, no! Emilio!"

Twelve

"YOU wanted to see me, Mrs. Gordon?" Michelle tried to keep her voice from trembling. *Please let Emilio be all right.*

"It's come to my attention that you went into Emilio Garcia's room without permission, even though Mrs. Davila specifically told you that only relatives are allowed in right now."

"I know, but I had a really good reason." Michelle wondered who'd ratted on her, the nurse—or Amber.

"Michelle, we don't make rules here in the hospital just to thwart you," said her father.

Michelle swung around at the sound of his voice. She hadn't heard him come in. "Dad, Emilio just realized he may lose his leg and his grandpa was released from the hospital. I thought I could help."

"We have a trained psychologist for that,"

he said. "I'm disappointed in you, Michelle. I thought you were learning to use your head, to think about the consequences of your actions. I see I was wrong."

"Unfortunately, Dr. De, this is the second time she's caused potential harm to a patient," Mrs. Gordon said. She told him about the medicine. "I know she's your daughter, but we do have to abide by the rules."

Michelle's stomach sank. "Does that mean I'm out of the program?"

"I'm afraid it does," Mrs. Gordon said. She cleared her throat and glanced uncomfortably at Michelle's father. "The first time you were careless and broke a rule, but this time you were clearly being defiant. Because we're short-handed, you may finish out the day. Turn in your badge this evening."

"I'm sorry, Michelle," her father said flatly, as if she were just anybody. He nodded to Mrs. Gordon, then walked out of the office.

Michelle hurried after him. "Wait! Dad, can't you do something? I promise I won't break any more rules."

"I've heard that too many times."

"But what about Emilio? If I'm not here—"

"I don't want to talk about it, Michelle.

I don't want to hear any more excuses or promises," he said.

"Dad, please don't let this change your mind about the Garcias maybe staying with us," Michelle said, barely able to meet her father's eyes.

"I talked to Mrs. Peterson about the Garcias and she was agreeable. I even started the wheels moving, but now—" He shook his head. "I'm not so sure it's a good idea. I think you've proven that you're much too irresponsible."

"Dad, please!"

But he turned away and headed toward his office.

Michelle felt as if he'd slammed a door on her. She wished her father would shout and lecture her. Anything would be better than the cold disapproval she could read in his face. The temptation to leave immediately was almost overwhelming, but it would be just more proof of her unreliability.

She found Travis in the lounge taking his break. "Well, you were right, Trav. I got bounced out of here."

"What are you talking about? What happened?"

"You warned me. I went into Emilio's room and I guess somebody saw me."

"Hey, I'm really sorry. I think you've been doing a great job."

Travis's beeper went off and a voice said, "Come to the desk. We have some flowers for 218."

Travis looked at her. "That's Gillespie. Why don't I take that call? You've had enough trauma for one day."

"No, that's okay," she said. "You're taking a break. I'll never see her again, anyhow."

Michelle took the flowers to Room 218. She paused at the door, wondering why she was bothering to subject herself to another of the woman's tirades. Was it out of a sense of responsibility to her father? It was probably dumb. He was never going to trust her again anyhow.

As usual, the TV was blaring. Mrs. Gillespie was leaning back against the pillows. Tears ran down her overpowdered cheeks. She took a tissue from the box beside her bed and dabbed at her eyes.

"Oh, no! She's going blind," Mrs. Gillespie said in a choked voice, "and he's not with her. She's all alone."

For a moment Michelle thought the woman was talking about a friend, but then realized she was crying over the movie on television.

Michelle shook her head. What could possibly be more ridiculous? But then she remembered Amber's story about the roses and love note. Maybe if you didn't have any friends or family, characters on television became real to you.

"Mrs. Gillespie? I have some flowers for you." She set them on a table.

The woman wiped her eyes again and turned toward Michelle. "You," she said. "Because of you, the nurse took away all my candy."

"I'm sorry. I just get nervous when people yell at me."

Mrs. Gillespie reached over for her purse and dug out a five-dollar bill. "Here, take this and get me a candy bar. No, get me three candy bars. Without nuts!"

Michelle shook her head. "You know you're not supposed to have sweets."

"What difference does it make? I'm going to die anyway. Now go get me that candy!"

"No. I won't help you kill yourself."

Mrs. Gillespie glared at her. "The other girl buys candy for me."

"You wouldn't mean Amber by any chance?"

"I think that was the name. Pretty girl. And not clumsy either. She'll get me the candy."

"I'll tell you what," Michelle said. "I'll go down to the cafeteria and get you a dietetic cookie."

Mrs. Gillespie made a face. "Blah! Might as well eat sawdust."

Trying to change the subject, Michelle reminded her about the flowers. "They're beautiful, aren't they?"

"Who are they from?"

"I don't know, but here's the card." Michelle tried to hand it over.

"No," she said, "you read it to me."

Michelle opened the card. "Dearest Beloved," she read aloud, "counting the days until I see you again. Until you return, the constellations will be dim and the flowers pale, and violins will not play in my heart."

Michelle glanced at Mrs. Gillespie. Her eyes were closed and her mouth was softened by a smile.

Amber was right, Michelle thought. Mrs. Gillespie must have told the florist what to put on the note. But she didn't let on. "It must be wonderful to have someone who cares about you that much," she said.

Mrs. Gillespie's face clouded. She shifted her attention to the television. "She's so brave," Mrs. Gillespie said of the actress on the screen. "It's terrible to be alone.

Alone in the dark."

She sniffled and used the tissue again. The movie ended and she clicked off the TV set. "Why do I watch that movie?" she said. "It always makes me feel the same way— terrible."

"I know," Michelle said. "For a long time after my mother died, I couldn't watch sad movies."

For the first time Mrs. Gillespie looked at her as if she were human. "How did your mama die?" she asked, her voice surprisingly soft.

Maybe talking about other people's problems helps her forget her own, Michelle thought. "She had cancer. My father's a doctor and he couldn't do anything to save her. Nothing."

Mrs. Gillespie nodded. "It was the same with my husband. They said it was incurable, but with the money he gave to this hospital, you'd think there would have been something they could do. If I'd have been able to be here with Herman, maybe things would have worked out differently."

"I'm almost sorry that I was here with Mom," Michelle said. "It was so hard to watch her slowly die."

Mrs. Gillespie ran her fingers over the

card. "I miss him so much. Even after all these years, it's as if he'll walk in here any moment and say 'Hi, Beautiful,' and rescue me from this place."

Michelle reached out and touched the woman's soft, puffy hand. "Your husband must have been very special."

"If only I'd been here," she whispered. "I never got to kiss him goodbye. I never got to hold his hand and tell him one last time how much I loved him." She looked at Michelle. "Don't ever forget to tell the ones you love how much you care for them. Sometimes . . ." Mrs. Gillespie blinked back tears. "Sometimes it's too late."

"I'm sure he knew," Michelle said gently. She was afraid to say too much for fear she'd make Mrs. Gillespie feel even worse. "I guess I'd better go now. We're short-handed."

"You'll come back, won't you? We could watch a funny movie together."

"I wish I could, but I won't be back anymore. I broke some rules and I won't be in the volunteer program after today."

"Rules! Pshaw! I break them every day, and they haven't kicked me out. I'll talk to Dr. De."

"That won't do much good. Dr. De Berg's

my dad. He's afraid I'll do something to hurt a patient," Michelle said bitterly.

"Don't you worry, my dear." With a determined look, Mrs. Gillespie sat up in bed. "Get me a nurse." She pointed at the flowers. "And give those to someone who doesn't have any. Never mind, just get me a wheelchair and I'll do it myself."

When Michelle just stood there, Mrs. Gillespie waved her hand. "Shoo, girl. I have work to do."

"You'd better take it easy."

"That's all I've been doing," Mrs. Gillespie said.

As she left, Michelle couldn't help smiling. Mrs. Gillespie was like a lemon pie. Once you got past her crusty exterior and her acid tongue, she was soft, and almost sweet inside.

Instead of looking for Travis, Michelle hunted down Amber. She found her hiding out in the lounge, watching television.

Amber looked up. "I didn't know you were still hanging around," she said. "I heard you got booted out of the program."

"You won, Amber. You don't need to gloat."

"Now, why would I gloat?"

"You couldn't wait to get me out of here.

I may have broken some rules because I wanted to help someone, but you don't really care anything about the patients. You buy candy for a diabetic when you know she could go into shock. You're a disgrace to the volunteer program."

"Oh, really? You're the one who's leaving," Amber said sarcastically. "Not me."

"Amber, one of these days people will wise up to you. I hope they do before someone gets hurt."

Amber sputtered something.

"Oh, and by the way," Michelle continued, "you're supposed to take an oversized wheelchair to Mrs. Gillespie."

Thirteen

DURING dinner that evening, Michelle and her father ate in silence. "How about if the two of us go to the beach tomorrow?" he said finally, trying to sound as if nothing had happened at the hospital.

Michelle was still too hurt and angry to make up. "I told you that I promised to stay at Dana's grandmother's place the whole weekend," she said flatly. "We'll be pretty busy."

"I know I said it was all right, but I think you should stay home, at least tonight."

"Why? Mrs. Weiser, next-door, always keeps an eye out when Dana's there alone. You're just afraid I'll break the rules!"

"Michelle, that's not fair. I had to treat you the same way I'd have treated anybody else."

"You didn't even listen to why I broke a rule. Doesn't it make any difference that I was trying to help Emilio?" Michelle pushed aside her plate. She had barely touched her food. "Is it all right if I go now? Or maybe you should just lock me in my room."

"I know you're angry, but you're not looking at my side. You can go, but we really need to talk about this."

"What's the point? You don't trust me to do anything right. It's not just today. You don't want me to go to Hawaii or anyplace else. You treat me like a baby." Michelle added the cruelest thing she could think of. "I wish Mom were here. She'd trust me." Then she stalked out of the dining room. "Mom would be on my side!"

Michelle ran to her room and hastily packed a bag. As she was leaving, her father asked, "Want me to drive you?"

"No, thanks," she said in an icy voice. "I'll ride my bike."

He sighed. "All right." He came over to her and bent his head as if he were going to kiss her on the cheek.

As Michelle averted her face, she saw the hurt in his eyes, but steeled herself against it. "Goodbye, Dad." With her back stiff, she walked down the front steps.

"Goodnight, sweetheart," he said softly. "I love you."

She wanted to turn around and run back to him, tell him that she loved him too, but she was too hurt.

Irritably, Michelle slung her bag over the handlebars and peddled as fast as she could along the road. Resentment still simmered inside her when she reached the gate of the mobile home park where Dana's grandmother lived.

The park, set in a grove of palms, was old, but all the homes and yards were well-kept. The town of Santa Reyes, like Palm Grove and Palm Springs, had many older people who had come to the desert to retire.

Michelle headed for the triple-wide mobile home where Dana's grandmother Francine lived. It looked like a regular house, except it was set on piers hidden by metal siding.

"Hello, Michelle."

She looked around and spotted Francine's next-door neighbor clipping a star jasmine bush. "Hi, Mrs. Weiser. Nice to see you again." She waved and ran up the steps of Francine's wide front porch. Before she could ring the bell, Dana opened the door.

"Are you psychic or something?"

Dana laughed. "No. I heard you talking to Mrs. Weiser. Francine just left for the airport, and Mom and Dad are hung up at a conference in Los Angeles. We can do anything we want." She gave Michelle a long look. "I still can't believe you got kicked out of the program. Are you okay?"

Michelle shrugged.

"Well, I think it stinks," Dana said.

"My head aches from thinking about this whole thing," said Michelle. "Let's talk about something else."

Francine's toy poodle started to whine, begging to be picked up. "Moon, you're spoiled rotten," Dana said. She lifted the dog and said to Michelle, "Come on in the kitchen while I feed him."

Michelle tossed her bag on the couch and followed. "Actually," she said, "I could stand to eat something, too—preferably not dog food. I only picked at my dinner."

As Dana opened a can of dog food and Michelle began to spread peanut butter on raisin bread, the phone rang.

Dana grabbed it on the second ring. "Oh, hi, Mom . . . yes, we're fine . . . sure, that's okay." She picked up a pencil and jotted something down. "Okay, we'll see you tomorrow. Don't worry about us. Mrs. Weiser will probably be here at dawn with fresh bagels and cream cheese . . . I'm not being sarcastic. I just wish she wouldn't hover. Michelle and I can take care of ourselves." There was a moment of silence while Dana just listened. Then she said, "Goodbye, Mom. Give Daddy a kiss for me."

"Parents!" Michelle said. "They'd keep us in diapers forever if they could."

"Their conference lasted longer than they thought," Dana said. "They're going to stay in a hotel tonight and head home in the morning."

"We could throw a party and only invite good-looking guys," Michelle said jokingly.

"Not with Mrs. Nosey next door. But speaking of good-looking guys, isn't it just our luck that Travis would ask us to go ice-skating tonight of all nights," Dana said.

"Well, it wasn't like a real date or anything. He was trying to round up a lot of other volunteers."

"I know, but it would have given us a chance to wear our leotards instead of those uniforms."

"After what happened today, I wouldn't have felt much like going anywhere," Michelle said. She yawned. The tension of the day had taken its toll. "I'm really beat."

Dana put Moon in his bed on the back porch. "Want to go for a swim?" she asked. "It'll cool us off."

"I'm too tired. Why don't we get into bed and watch TV or talk?" Michelle suggested.

"Sounds good to me. I have to lock up first," Dana said. "You know my grandmother."

Francine was scared of more things than Dana was. She had double locks on all the doors and ornamental bars on every window.

Michelle helped Dana, then got her bag and undressed. She settled into one of the twin beds. "Oh, this feels great," she said. "I can't believe how tired I am."

They watched TV for a while. The movie reminded Michelle of Mrs. Gillespie. "You know, I actually felt kind of sorry for her today. I think the only family she has are TV characters. I kind of know how she feels. I only have my dad."

"I'm glad I have lots of cousins and aunts and uncles. I just wish I didn't have to spend as much time with them as I do."

Michelle thought about how different she and Dana were. Dana wanted out of all the family things. Michelle was the opposite. What she wanted most was to be with her dad, and yet tonight she had pushed him away. The temptation to call and apologize was strong. Mrs. Gillespie's words came to mind: Don't wait too long to tell the person you love that you care.

Michelle glanced at the digital clock on the dresser, surprised at how many hours had fled. It was too late to call now. But first thing in the morning she would jump on the phone.

"I'm lucky I didn't have to go to L.A. with Mom and Dad," Dana was saying.

Michelle murmured something in return, but she could barely keep her eyes open. The drone of the air conditioner in the window and Dana's voice got fainter and fainter. She was hardly aware when Dana finally shut the TV off.

Michelle fell asleep thinking about her father. In her dreams he was angry with her. She kept trying to tell him she was sorry, but he wouldn't listen. He—

"Michelle!" Dana screamed. "Michelle!"

Michelle sat up, startled out of a sound sleep. The light came on and she blinked and shaded her eyes. "What's wrong?"

"Earthquake! Get up! We have to get out!"

"Take it easy, Dana. It couldn't have been much of a shake. It didn't even wake me up."

"Well, it woke me up. I'm scared." Dana's face was pale, and her voice shaky. "I'll never get back to sleep. I wish Francine were here."

"Hey, it's okay." Michelle glanced at the clock: 3:32. Morning was a long time off. "Let's go fix some hot chocolate. My mom used to do that whenever I had a bad dream."

"That was no dream. I felt it."

"I know, but the hot chocolate will help. Come on."

Dana put on slippers, but Michelle padded barefooted into the kitchen. She flicked on the light. "I'll get the milk. You find the cocoa, sugar, and a pan. I hope you have some marshmallows."

Michelle was taking the carton out of the refrigerator when she heard a rumble like a train coming toward them. A sudden, tremendous jolt knocked her against the sink. The floor bucked violently.

Dana screamed.

At the same moment, Michelle pitched forward onto her knees. Bottles and jars flew out of the refrigerator, a wall clock shot across the room, and cupboards flew open, sending dishes crashing. The horrifying noises collided with the sound of crashes from other rooms, and another piercing scream from Dana.

"I have to get out! I have to get out! I have to get *out*!"

"Dana! Get under the worktable!" Michelle cried, choking with fear. "Watch out for glass." Gritting her teeth, she began to make her own way toward the heavy butcher block worktable. Standing was impossible. She crawled as quickly as she could, wincing as a piece of glass nicked her leg. "Cover your face!"

The shaking seemed to go on and on and on, as if the entire earth were breaking apart. The floor heaved convulsively and tipped to one side. Two metal piers shot up through the floor like spears, barely missing Michelle. Finally, she made it to the table and gripped one of the wooden legs to keep from sliding back toward the refrigerator.

Suddenly the lights went out. The building gave one last shudder.

Blackness. The silence was deafening.

Michelle fumbled for Dana, and pulled her under the table. Dana's breath was loud and fast.

"We're going to die!" Dana cried. "We're going to die!"

"It's over." Michelle's heart thundered so hard she felt as if it would burst. She tried to keep her voice steady. "We're okay."

The girls clung together, too frightened to move, too awed by what had just happened to their world. Although the air was stifling, they both shivered violently, as if the quake tremors had penetrated their bodies.

"It's okay, it's okay." Michelle forced aside her own panic, trying to reassure Dana.

A shrill ring startled her and she let out a scream. When it rang again, she tried to laugh. "It's the phone. It's just the phone."

Dana kept whimpering as if she hadn't heard the ringing. "We're going to die!"

Michelle pushed to her feet. She wished she could see where the broken glass lay. She wished she could see anything.

Disoriented, she groped toward the wall phone, grateful that one thing, anyway, still worked. Once, she stumbled over a stool, sending cans rolling. The phone rang again, the sound guiding her.

"Don't hang up!" she yelled. Knowing that someone was on the other end of the line made her feel less alone. "Please don't hang up!"

She finally reached the phone. "Hello! Hello!"

"Michelle, are you two girls all right?" Mrs. Weiser sounded breathless.

"I guess so."

"Do you smell gas?"

Michelle sniffed the air. "I can't smell anything but dill pickles. Everything came out of the fridge."

"Grab some food and water, then get out of the kitchen," Mrs. Weiser instructed. "It's the most dangerous room. And see if you can quickly find a blanket. There will be some aftershocks and you might not be able to get back inside. Hurry. I'll meet you girls out front."

Michelle had barely hung up when the phone rang again. This time it was her father. At the sound of his calm voice, she began to cry.

"Honey, are you hurt?"

"No, Dana and I are okay. Mrs. Weiser told us to get outside."

"You stay with her. I have to get to the hospital. Mookie and the house are safe. I'll try to get there as soon as I can."

"Dad, I have to tell you—"

The line went dead and Michelle dropped the receiver. Just then, the floor began to shake again. Dana's scream sent a prickle up Michelle's neck. She braced herself against the wall, but the aftershock lasted only a few seconds.

"Dana, come help me," she called out,

hoping that if her friend was busy she wouldn't be so scared. "Find some water and food."

A reddish glow from outside filtered into the mobile home. It provided just enough light for Michelle to make it to the bedroom. The dresser had overturned. Clothes were flung everywhere. Lamps lay overturned and broken. Michelle slid into shoes, grabbed a blanket, and hurried back to the kitchen. She tried the back door, but it was jammed. "We can't get Moon from this side—"

A violent jolt cut her off.

Michelle heard Dana running toward the front door and the sound of broken glass crunching under her feet.

As Michelle started to pick up an unbroken jar of peanut butter and a box of crackers that had fallen from the cupboard, she heard a scream and a crash. She raced to the front door and started to step out onto the front porch—only there was no porch.

"Dana!"

Fourteen

MICHELLE looked wildly around. Down the street a mobile home was ablaze. The red glare from it lit up the night. Residents shouted and carried buckets of water from the pool. In a panic, Michelle screamed, "Dana! Where are you?"

She heard a moan and looked down. Dana lay among broken steps and ruptured porch.

The left side of the porch was still intact. As Michelle was climbing down, Barney, the maintenance man, came running across the street. He carried a big wrench and a flashlight. "Is everyone okay over here?"

"No! We need help!"

Barney lifted Dana out of the rubble and laid her on the blanket Michelle had brought out. Her heart racing, Michelle knelt beside her friend. "Is she okay? Is she hurt bad? What'll I do?"

"The first thing you do is calm down," Barney told her. "I think Dana's just stunned and scared, and maybe in shock." He looked around. "Where's Francine. Is she all right?"

"She's at a golf tournament," Michelle said. "We're house-sitting." She looked at the mobile home, half-off its supports, and began to laugh hysterically. "We didn't do a very good job."

Barney gave her shoulder a little shake. "Come on, girl. There's too much to do to lose your cool."

Michelle took a deep breath. "Maybe I should try to call Francine and the Changs."

"You can't," said Mrs. Weiser, coming out to join them. "The phones are all out."

Dana sat up slowly and ran her hands over her legs and arms. "I guess I didn't break anything."

Michelle put her arms around her friend. "It's over, Dana," she said, trying to sound calm. "We made it through."

"If you three are okay, I'll check on the other folks," Barney said. He picked up the wrench and flashlight. "Nearly every home is off its foundation." He sniffed the air. "I smell smoke close by. Is everything turned off inside?"

"I can't remember." Michelle felt disoriented, as if she were in a terrible dream.

They moved around to the side of the house. Barney flashed his light across the building.

"Look!" Michelle cried and pointed to the bedroom window.

The air-conditioning unit outside the window had broken loose. While the power was still on, sparks from the loose wires had started a fire.

"I'll get the hose!" Michelle said. Her voice didn't even sound like her own.

"No! Water will make it worse!" Barney told her. "If you're okay, go for help. I'll go get a fire extinguisher."

"Moon!" Dana cried. "I forgot all about him!" She stood. "I've got to get him—"

"No!" Barney said sharply. "Stay away from there until we get the fire under control."

Dana did an about-face and ran to the front of the mobile home. Before they could stop her she had scrambled up on the broken porch.

"Dana! Get back here," Michelle yelled. "The whole place could go up in flames!"

"Francine will kill me if Moon is hurt," Dana called over her shoulder.

"She'd rather lose the dog than you," Mrs. Weiser hollered. "Don't go in there."

"I'll get the gas turned off," Barney said. He ran toward the back.

"Mrs. Weiser, you go for help." Michelle took the flashlight from her. "I'm going after Dana. It's pitch dark in—"

A violent jolt stopped her. The ground heaved. She heard a crash from inside. "Dana!" she screamed.

The ground stopped moving. After a quick glance to see that Mrs. Weiser was already on her way to get help, Michelle headed for the porch. The last jolt had forced the door closed. Michelle strained against it, but it refused to give. Panicked, she ran around to the side of the mobile home, looking for a window to climb in. Her heart sank. There was no way she could get through the ornamental bars.

The flames were growing stronger and spreading swiftly toward the front of the house. Michelle raced back to the porch. The door was open a crack now and she could see Dana's hand.

"Can you open the door any wider?" Michelle asked her.

"The bookcase fell against it. I can't get out!"

"Barney, come help me!"

When he didn't answer, Michelle put her back against the door and pushed as hard as she could. It moved only an inch or two. "Can you open the window bars from the inside?"

"I can't get up. I've hurt my foot. Michelle!" she shrieked. "Flames! I'm going to burn!"

Frantically, Michelle threw herself against the door. This time it opened a little wider. "Try to squeeze through!" she yelled. "You can do it."

Dana managed to get a shoulder through the opening, then sank back. "I can't." She was coughing now. "I can't."

Michelle heard sounds of running feet and turned to see Mrs. Weiser. She was surprised to see Travis with her. "Dana's stuck!" she cried.

Travis scrambled up on the porch. Together, he and Michelle both hit the door. It moved inward several more inches. "Now try to squeeze through," Travis told Dana.

"I—can't," she said in a choked voice. "Smoke . . ."

In the distance, a siren wailed. Barney came running toward them, carrying Moon. He handed the dog to Mrs. Weiser and quickly surveyed the situation.

"She's trapped!" Michelle screamed. "We have to get her out of there fast!"

The three of them put their shoulders to the door. "Get back out of the way," Barney told Dana. "One, two, three, hit!"

This time the door moved enough for Barney and Travis to pull Dana through the opening. Her pale face was streaked with dirt. They carried her to the blanket. Mrs. Weiser checked Dana's ankle. "I think it's just a slight sprain."

"Dana, don't ever do a stupid thing like that again!" Michelle said, hugging her friend tightly. "I'm sorry to yell. I was just so scared for you."

Travis exhaled slowly, and pushed a lock of hair out of his eyes. He gave Michelle and Dana a quick smile.

"I'd forgotten you only lived across the road," Michelle said to him. "How did you happen to come over?"

"I knew these older mobile homes would take a beating. Actually, I came to see if I could help—and make sure you two were okay before I go to the hospital."

Suddenly Michelle realized she was still in her pajamas and must look awful. She tried to smooth her hair as she said,

"Thanks. I don't know when I've been so scared."

The siren stopped, but Michelle could hear the heavy rumble of the fire truck as it made its way through debris. As firefighters set to work putting out the blaze, a paramedic taped Dana's ankle. People congregated in groups, listening to transistor radios and talking in breathless, excited voices.

"Worst one I've ever felt, and I've lived here forty-odd years."

"I was up in the high desert during the 7.6 quake. This one had to be as big."

"I was in a 6.0 up north. They say a 7.0 is a hundred times larger than a 6.0, and I believe it."

"It's amazing no one was killed in the park. I'm going to stay in my car."

"We could be without power and water for several days," said one woman. "I keep telling myself I should stock up on water and food and be prepared, but . . ." She sighed. "We always have such good intentions."

When the fire was out, the truck proceeded down the street, checking on all the homes. Although there were no large jolts, the ground periodically shook. Each time,

Michelle braced herself, waiting for a big one to hit.

"I'm going over to the hospital in a few minutes," Travis said. "When the hospital called my dad, they said Palm Grove got hit hard."

"I'll go with you. Poor Emilio must be scared to death."

The sky was turning pink over the eastern mountains. Dawn was quickly approaching. A layer of dust covered the park like a thick brown cloud. The park looked like pictures of towns in a war zone.

Michelle turned to Dana. ""You'll be okay here with Mrs. Weiser. I'm just going in to change out of my pajamas."

"You told me I was crazy for going back inside," Dana said.

"The fire's out now, and I can't go to the hospital like this." Without letting Dana argue her out of it, Michelle climbed up on the porch and squeezed through the narrow opening.

When she stepped inside, she shivered. The smell of smoke and burned wood clung to the air. Her heart pounded wildly, and for a moment she couldn't catch her breath.

Now that it was getting lighter, the damage showed plainly. The living room was trashed. Everything was on the floor. The kitchen was even worse. Michelle skidded on the wet floor. The refrigerator had moved a foot from the wall. The microwave was smashed. What the quake hadn't damaged, fire and water had finished. Oddly, none of the windows were broken.

Nauseated and lightheaded, Michelle hurried to the bathroom and retched, but nothing came up. The heavy porcelain toilet lid looked as if it had been flung across the room. The shower door hung at an angle.

As quickly as she could, Michelle made her way into the bedroom and changed into the jeans and T-shirt she'd worn the day before. She looked around for something to bring Dana. All of the dresser drawers were on the floor, and the overturned dresser was blocking the closet. Finally, Michelle grabbed Dana's robe, which had somehow managed to stay on the foot of the bed.

Back in the kitchen she found a plastic jug of water, then rummaged through the mess on the floor and uncovered some cans of soda and juice.

A sharper aftershock hit, rattling the unbroken windows. Michelle nearly dropped the water. Suddenly the walls seemed to close in on her and she hurried to get out.

"Sorry, I couldn't get to any of your clothes," she said to Dana a moment later, handing her the robe. "This was the best I could do."

"I'm going with you and Travis," Dana said firmly. "I don't care if I'm in a robe or a bathing suit. I can do something to help."

"You can help plenty," Travis said. "All the doctors and nurses will bring their kids to the hospital. They'll need babysitters."

"I don't think you children should leave here," Mrs. Weiser said. "There are probably wires down, and heaven knows what the streets are like."

"We'll be careful," Travis assured her. "And the hospital's probably the safest building around."

"Take care of Moon for me," Dana said. "If Mom and Dad can get a call through, tell them where I am."

"I left my car outside the park," Travis said. "Do you think you can walk on that ankle?" he asked Dana.

"It hurts a little, but I can make it."

With Travis on one side, and Michelle on the other, they helped Dana to the car. Michelle climbed into the front, while Travis got Dana settled in the back where she could put her legs up.

The highway from Santa Reyes to Palm Grove was dotted with small businesses, restaurants, and trailer parks. The closer they got to Palm Grove, the more visible the destruction. Nearly every building had lost its windows. Travis turned on the radio and tuned to a station reporting about the quake.

"The largest earthquake to hit southern California since the Landers 7.6 struck at 3:38 this morning with a magnitude of 7.3," the radio announcer's voice said. "Cal Tech is estimating that the epicenter is near the resort town of Palm Grove. Damage is likely to be considerable. The biggest worry, although seismologists are playing it down, is how close this quake is to the San Andreas Fault. If one hits along—"

Dana gave a little moan and Travis switched off the radio.

Michelle began to tremble. She felt as if all the blood had drained out of her body. She couldn't stop shaking. "What's wrong with me?" she cried.

"It's probably just a delayed reaction," Travis said. "I was surprised at how calm you were before."

"I guess you're right. As long as I was busy, I was—Travis, watch out!"

"I see it," Travis said. The car squealed to a stop.

Debris and bricks from a fallen building and a downed power pole had almost hidden the huge fissure in the road. The pavement had buckled and dropped two or three feet. A deep crack continued across the road and on as far as they could see.

Travis backed the car up. "We'll have to find a way around this."

Dana grabbed Michelle's shoulder. "What if there's another quake? What if the earth opens up and swallows the car?"

"The aftershocks shouldn't be as strong," Michelle said, trying to sound confident. It was hard to be calm when your insides were churning and you could hardly catch your breath.

They saw an ambulance making its way down a side street, its siren wailing.

"It looks like it's heading for the hospital," Travis said. "I'll follow it. They're really going to need our help."

Finally, they made it to the hospital and Travis pulled into the parking lot. Everywhere she looked, Michelle saw controlled chaos. Although it was light now, outdoor floodlights and headlights of cars illuminated the area. Doctors and nurses were tending to people, sorting out which patients needed attention first.

Michelle jumped out of the car and searched for her father. She spotted a doctor she recognized and ran over to him. "Dr. Fisher! Do you know where my dad is? I have to see him!"

Dr. Fisher momentarily glanced up from the patient he was examining. "I'm afraid he's in surgery, Michelle."

She groaned, unable to conceal her disappointment. "I really need to talk to him, but I suppose he'll be busy there for hours."

Dr. Fisher straightened up. He touched her shoulder. "Honey, you don't understand. Your dad's not *doing* surgery. He's *in* surgery. He was hurt in a car accident coming to the hospital."

Fifteen

"**N**O!" Michelle cried. "How bad is—" She couldn't get the words out.

"We don't know yet," the doctor said. "It's a madhouse here. I'm sorry I can't tell you anything else, Michelle."

"Doctor Fisher! Come quick!" a nurse called. "I've got a man here who's started to hemorrhage!"

"I'll try to find out more," he called as he hurried away.

Michelle ran toward the hospital. Tears blurred her eyes and she could hardly see.

Please, not again. Not like Mom. I won't have anybody. Please let him be all right. I'll do anything if he doesn't die. I haven't told him I'm sorry. I haven't told him I love him.

Travis and Dana caught up with her. "You look sick," Dana said, putting her arm around Michelle's shoulder. "Are you okay?"

"It's my dad. He's hurt, and I have to see him."

Mrs. Gordon rushed out the emergency door and hurried over. She wore a robe and slippers, and her face was harried. "Thank heaven, you're here. We have hysterical children and most of the parents haven't been able to get here yet. Come along!"

"I can't," Michelle said. "I have to see my dad. He's been in a car accident."

"I know. He's in surgery," Mrs. Gordon said. "You can't see him yet. I don't mean to seem insensitive, but this is your job. We need you."

"But I'm not—"

"You've had some experience," Mrs. Gordon broke in. "We need you now."

"It'll take your mind off your dad," Dana said. "You can't do anything for him now. They'll take good care of him."

Like they did my mother? Michelle thought.

"Come on," Mrs. Gordon said briskly, more like her usual self. "Travis and Dana, get your uniforms and go to the children's wing. Michelle, you go to the conference room. Woody needs help. Most of the staff brought in their own children."

Michelle hesitated. Maybe she couldn't

see her father while he was in surgery, but she wanted to be there—just in case. . . . She pushed the thought away. *He's going to be okay, he's going to be okay.* She had to try not to think the worst.

"I'll see you two later," she said to Travis and Dana.

The conference room was noisy with kids yelling and babies crying. Michelle spotted Woody holding a small child.

"Hi, Woody," she said, "I'm here to help."

"Honey, I heard about your dad," he said. He put a hand on her shoulder. "It'll help if you keep busy."

"I hope so," she said, trying to keep from crying.

"Try to round up the hyper kids and play some games. Encourage them to talk about what happened."

Michelle gathered some of the younger children and sat them down in a circle. "Were you guys as scared as I was?" she asked, hoping they wouldn't sense how upset she was. "That was some shaker, huh?"

Several of the children started talking about their experiences. One girl began to cry. Words poured out in a rush. "It was so dark and scary quiet," she said. "I couldn't find Mommy and Daddy. Me and my dog—

his name is Frosty—we had to crawl out through the doggy door."

A boy piped up, "I got thrown out of bed! The floor was going up and down, up and down. That was real scary."

Michelle nodded and turned to another little girl. "Hi," she said softly. "What about you?"

"Her name's Amy," said the boy. He blinked solemnly. "She doesn't talk much."

Amy sucked her thumb and stared at the floor. "I want my mama," she whimpered. "Where's my mama?"

"She'll be here when she's through helping hurt people," Michelle said calmly. She put the child on her lap. "You're safe here."

A few minutes later Woody came over and whispered, "How's it going, Michelle?"

"Okay, I guess. Have you heard anything about my dad?"

"No, but as soon as some more help gets here, you can go to surgery and see what you can find out." He handed her some crayons and paper. "Get them to draw pictures—how they felt about the earthquake. I'm not a psychologist, but it's been my experience that it helps."

Michelle passed out the papers and

crayons. Amy clung to her and wouldn't let go. "Here," Michelle said, giving the little girl some crayons. "You can help me."

Amy shook her head and sucked her thumb. Wherever Michelle went, Amy followed, even when Michelle had to go to the rest room.

She was reading a story to a group of children when she heard a commotion from the doorway. She turned to see Mrs. Gillespie and two other patients wheeling their chairs into the room.

"All right, Woody, what do you want us to do?" Mrs. Gillespie said. "We're here to help."

"What's got into her?" Woody whispered to Michelle.

"Beats me," Michelle said with a grateful smile. She might be out of the program, but she hadn't done everything wrong.

"Mrs. Gillespie, how are you at storytelling?" Woody asked.

"Humph! Who do you think was the real Mother Goose?" she said with a grin. "I have a million stories."

Michelle waited until Woody got Mrs. Gillespie started, then asked, "Now that we have more help, is it okay if I go up and see Emilio?"

"Sure," he said. "Thanks for pitching in.

You did a great job."

Michelle picked up her little shadow. "Amy, I have to go take care of some sick children." She pointed to a toddler who had just come in. "I'll bet she's scared. Why don't you go talk to her. She could use a friend."

Reluctantly, Amy relaxed her grip on Michelle. "Okay. But if you see my mama, you tell her I want to go home."

Michelle took the steps two at a time. Before she went to the children's wing, she stopped at the surgery waiting room. Mrs. Covington was at the desk.

"Remember me?" she said to the senior volunteer. "I'm Michelle De Berg. Is there any word about my dad? Is he out of surgery yet?"

"Of course I remember you, Michelle. I'm sorry about your father. Without phones, it's hard to get information. The last I heard, Dr. De was in surgery or waiting to go in."

Michelle struggled to hold back the tears. "I hate this waiting. If you hear anything, will you try to get the information to the children's wing? I'll be helping out there."

Mrs. Covington nodded. "Try not to worry, dear."

Try not to worry. Why did people always say that?

In the children's section, Mrs. Davila was helping Travis move beds.

"We're doubling up," Mrs. Davila said. "Partly to make it easier for us and partly so the children have company. It's scary to be alone."

"How can I help?"

Mrs. Davila wearily brushed back her hair. "Mostly, just be with the kids and give them a lot of hugging and comforting."

"Is it okay if I look in on Emilio?"

"As soon as he awakens, I want you to talk to him. He asks about you all the time."

"Thanks. I'm really worried about him. Mrs. Davila, my dad's been hurt. He's in surgery. If you find out anything about him, will you let me know?"

"Of course I will." She gave Michelle a reassuring smile.

For the next few hours Michelle was so busy she hardly had time to think about her father. During her volunteer training, she had thought some of the things she had to do were useless and dumb, but not anymore.

Finally, she found a free moment to peek in on Emilio. He was still asleep. As always, he looked small and vulnerable, but his face was no longer flushed and feverish-looking.

"Is he awake?" Mrs. Davila asked, coming up behind her.

Emilio moaned in his sleep.

"He's stirring," Michelle whispered. "His color looks better, don't you think?"

"If he continues to improve, I think we're going to save his leg," Mrs. Davila said.

"I was afraid he wouldn't be able to throw off the infection. I'd give anything if I could help him."

"I know you got into trouble for going into his room the other day. Rules make things easier, but sometimes we forget that people come first. Whatever you said or did, it helped that little boy. I wouldn't be at all surprised to see you get your badge back." Mrs. Davila smiled. "Last night, Mrs. Gillespie read the riot act to Mrs. Gordon, your dad, and just about everybody she could think of."

"I appreciate her help, but I don't know if Mrs. Gordon or my dad will ever trust me again. I feel awful about it."

Mrs. Davila nodded, encouraging Michelle to continue.

"But today . . . I really felt I was doing something important, really helping people." Michelle even understood her dad a little better. You couldn't help everyone—like her mother. So you tried to save those who could be saved. "I think I know now how my dad feels about being a doc—"

She stopped at a sound from Emilio. His breathing had changed.

"He's waking up," Mrs. Davila said.

Michelle drew close to the boy. "Emilio?" she whispered.

He opened his eyes but cringed against the pillow.

"Hey," she said, "It's me, Mich—"

She paused when he looked up. His eyes were wide and blank, like Orphan Annie's.

"Emilio, honey, it's okay. It's okay." Michelle sat on the bed and pulled him into her arms. She could feel him trembling. "You're okay now. You're safe with me."

"Gramps. I want Gramps!"

"He'll be here as soon as he can," she assured him.

Emilio started to cry. The tough, strong kid was just a scared little boy.

For a long time Michelle just held him, murmuring, "You're okay. I won't let anything happen to you."

When he finally stopped shaking, she tried to get him to talk. "Boy," she said, "that old Earthquake Monster really went crazy last night, didn't he?"

"There ain't no monster."

"I know. I used to be scared of thunder. I know there aren't any giants either, but my mom told me that they were bowling in the sky. I didn't really believe her. But thinking about that made the thunder less scary."

Dana came into the room. "Heard anything about your dad yet?"

Michelle shook her head. "No, but keeping busy has helped."

"Mrs. Davila said she wants to move Emilio next door with some other boys."

"I don't wanna go," Emilio said. "Gramps won't find me."

"I'll put a note on the door," Michelle told him.

"You do not need to," Mr. Garcia said. "I am here."

"Gramps!" Emilio cried. "I was scared you was hurt."

"The shelter didn't get much damage. I hitched a ride here to see you." Mr. Garcia searched Emilio's face. "You are all right?" he asked.

"Sure I am," Emilio said stoutly. "Earthquakes don't scare me none."

Michelle had to smile. His tough facade was in place again. "I have a T-shirt for you, Emilio," she told him. "It says: 'It's Not My

Fault.' Get it? Earthquake Fault."

When Emilio didn't smile, she said lamely, "I'll bring it to you during visiting hours tomorrow." She hated to tell him, but it wasn't fair for him to hear it from someone else. "Emilio, I might not be working here at the hospital anymore."

"You're comin' back!" he said in a panicky voice.

"Sure I am. I'll visit you every day. And if I have my way, when you're out of here—" She stopped. She couldn't tell him or Mr. Garcia until she was sure.

"Michelle," Travis called from the door. "I just talked to my dad. He was the anesthesiologist during your dad's surgery. Your dad's in the recovery room."

Michelle felt her heart leap. *Thank you. Thank you.* "He was in there so long. Are you sure he's—is he going to make it?"

"He lost a lot of blood before he got here. It was touch and go for a while, but he wasn't in surgery all that time. He wouldn't let anyone work on him until everybody else was taken care of."

That was her dad, all right.

"You'd better get there right away," Travis said.

Michelle bolted from the room, raced past

Mrs. Davila and started down the hall, then stopped. "It's okay if I go, isn't it?"

"Of course. You stay with him as long as they'll let you."

When she got to the recovery room, Michelle hesitated outside the door.

"Are you Michelle De Berg?" a nurse asked.

She nodded. "How is he? Is it okay if I go in?"

"For a minute or so. You're the best medicine he can get right now. Just don't tire him."

The recovery room was full of patients. Michelle found her father in an alcove full of equipment. His head and chest were bandaged. His left arm was in a cast.

She rushed over to his bed and knelt beside it. "Daddy! I was so afraid. . . ." She began to cry. "I thought you had died."

"A few broken bones and a ruptured spleen won't keep me down."

"After I heard you'd been hurt, I was afraid I'd never see you again. I lost Mom. I thought—" Michelle's voice broke. "I was afraid I'd lost you too."

Her father reached out and touched Michelle's hair. "You're so much like her, baby. I feel guilty because I haven't always been there for you. I don't know how to be both a mother and a father."

"But Dad, Mom's not here any more. And we can't bring her back. What I want is a father," Michelle said softly. "Daddy, what I have—what I need—is you."

About the Author

Alida E. Young lives with her husband in the high desert of southern California. When she's not researching or writing a new novel, she enjoys taking long walks. To help her write her novels, she likes to put herself in the shoes of her characters, to try to feel things the way they would.

In writing *Earthquake!*, Alida called on experts for information, but she also drew on her own experiences. "Some earthquakes are small and you don't feel them at all. But during the big earthquake in 1992, I felt like I was on a bucking horse. I was standing at my desk and I had to hold on for dear life just to keep my balance. It only went on for about 45 seconds, but it felt like a lifetime."

Alida's books have made her an award-winning author. In 1990 her novel *Too Young to Die* was named a winner in the national Book-It! competition.

Other Willowisp books by Alida include *Is My Sister Dying?*, *Dead Wrong*, *Summer Cruise*, *Summer Love*, and the popular *Megan the Klutz* books. She has also written adventure novels, including *Terror in the Tomb of Death* and *Return to the Tomb of Death*.

Earthquake! is her seventeenth book for Willowisp Press.